Readers in Residence Answer Key

Volume 1

Sleuth

by Debra Bell, PhD

apologia

Apologia Educational Ministries, Inc.

READERS IN RESIDENCE ANSWER KEY, VOLUME 1

Published by
Apologia Educational Ministries
1106 Meridian Plaza, Suite 220/340
Anderson, Indiana 46016
www.apologia.com

Manufactured in the USA
First Printing: August 2016

ISBN: 978-1-940110-85-1

Cover Design: Doug Powell
Book Design: Holly Grundon

Printed by Bang Printing, Brainerd, MN

Contents

Note: No answer key is required for units 2, 4, and 6 (modules 5, 10, and 14).

How to use this Answer Key

Your children have learned to read.

NOW IT'S TIME FOR THEM TO READ TO LEARN.

This Answer Key is your road map to using *Readers in Residence*, volume 1. You will find all the tools you need to do the following:

make a daily schedule

Suggested Daily Schedule

Week	Day 1	Day 2	Day 3	Day 4
7	Module 4 4.5 - 4.7	Module 4 4.8 - 4.10	Module 4 4.11	Module 4 4.12 - 4.13
8	Module 4 4.14	Module 4 4.15	Module 4 4. 16 Unit Project	Module 4 4.16 Unit Project
9	Module 4	Module 4 Checklist 4	**Intro to Unit 2** Read Unit 2 Introduction. Pick your book.	Module 5 5.1 - 5.4
		...lule 5 ...d OYO Book - ...- 5.8)	Module 5 Read OYO Book - (5.7 - 5.8)	Module 5 Read OYO Book - (5.7 - 5.8)
		...lule 5 ...- 5.12	Module 5 5.13 - 5.14	Module 5 5.15 - 5.16
12	Module 5 5.17 - 5.18	Module 5 5.19 - Checklist 5	**Intro to Unit 3** Read Unit 3 Introduction. Study the unit project rubric.	Module 6 Reader's Questions - 6.3
13	Module 6 6.4 - Meet the Illustrator	Module 6 6.5 - 6.7	Module 6 6.8 - 6.9	Module 6 6.10
14	Module 6 6.11 - 6.12	Module 6 6.13 - 6.15	Module 6 6.16 - 6.17	Module 6 6.18 - 6.19

explain assignments

2.8 Read *Sarah, Plain and Tall*: Chapter 2

Directions: Read chapter 2 of *Sarah, Plain and Tall*. What do you learn about Sarah from her letters? Use the chart on the next page to list what you learn and what you expect Sarah to be like when she arrives at the Wittings' home. We've provided the first clue for you.

Answers will vary. Sample answers are provided.

Clues in Sarah's Letters

What I Learn about Sarah from Her Letter to Anna	What I Expect Sarah to Be Like Based on Her Letter to Anna	What I Learn about Sarah from Her Letter to Caleb	What I Expect Sarah to Be Like Based on Her Letter to Caleb
Sarah can braid hair, bake bread, and make stew.	She is capable.	She has a c... Seal.	
She prefers to build and paint.	She may not enjoy the tasks women typically do.	She says... likes do... the time...	
Her favorite colors are the colors of the sea.	She loves where she lives. She will miss her home.	She says... house s...	...make an effort to like her new home.
She has a brother named William who is a fisherman.	She admires him. She will miss him. She will talk about her family and home.	She can keep a fire going at night.	She is capable. She will know how to help around the house.
She has sent a book of sea birds.	She is thoughtful. She likes to give gifts. She wants Anna to know about her life.	She says that she doesn't think she snores because "Seal has never told" her.	She likes to tease. She sees the humor in things.

keep track of progress

Checklist for Module 1

Directions: When you have completed a task, make a ✔ in the "Done" column. Ask a parent, teacher, or reading coach to award you points for each task using the checklist point system. Fill in the points you have earned on the Sleuth's Log in the appendix.

Tasks	Done ✔	Points Earned
1.4 Nonfiction or Fiction • List examples of nonfiction and fiction books that you have in your home.		
...ve ...ave in your		
...rary that ...the chart		
...each book ...you notice ...ing coach.		
...ction ...of a historical fiction book with a parent, teacher, or reading coach.		
1.9 The Cover of *Sarah, Plain and Tall* (*SPT*) • Answer the questions by using the clues you find on the front and back covers of the book.		
1.10 Clues to Genre • Write your best ideas for answers to these questions.		
• Discuss your answers to the questions with a parent, teacher, or reading coach.		

Checklist Point System:

1–6 points may be awarded by a parent, teacher, or reading coach for each task completed. Here are the recommended guidelines:

6 – exemplary in quality *and* effort

5 – exemplary in either quality *or* effort

4 – acceptable in quality *and* effort

3 – acceptable in either quality *or* effort

2 – needs improvement in quality *and* effort

1 – incomplete

Continued on next page »

evaluate your child's work

Rubric Point System:

5 points – This part of the project is outstanding.

4 points – This part of the project is very strong.

3 points – This part of the project shows a lot of effort.

2 points – This part of the project needs improvement.

1 point – This part of the project is missing.

Rubric for Unit 1 Project

Traits of Good Character Development	Points Earned
Physical Traits • I have described some of my main character's physical traits.	
Character Traits • I have described how I will show what my character is like through what he or she says.	
• I have described how I will show what my character is like through what he or she does.	
• I have described how I will s... character is like through wh... him or her.	
Conflict • I have described a significan... character faces in the story.	
Response • I have described how my cha... the significant problem he or s...	
Changes • I have described how my character changes because of the significant problem he or she faces.	
• I have described how I will show this change through what my character learns, says, does, or thinks.	
Quality • I have created a complete project with the required elements.	

Answers

This Answer Key contains answers or sample answers for the following student activities from the Student Text and Workbook:

- activities where one correct answer is required
- activities where answers may vary, but a set range of answers is acceptable
- activities where the student is asked to give examples
- activities where the student is asked to make an inference

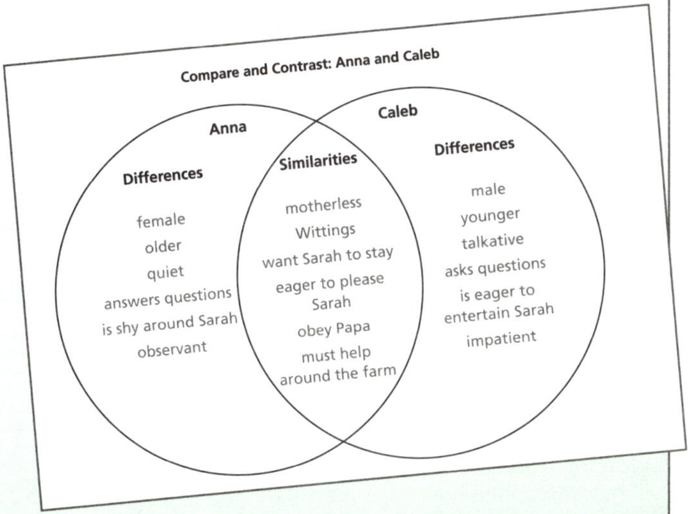

6.11 Reading Strategies: Denotations and Connotations of Words

Directions: On the next two pages, study the following sentences from *Charlotte's Web*. First, think of the images and experiences that you picture when you read the underlined word. Then decide what emotions you associate with the word and write them on the line provided. Finally, circle whether the connotations of the word are positive, negative, or neutral. Discuss your answers with a parent, teacher, or reading coach.

Answers will vary. Sample answers are provided. Further explanation for why the word has positive, negative, or neutral connotations is also provided.

1. "A weakling makes trouble." (page 3)

   Images and experiences I picture when I read this word: someone getting beaten up, someone who is sickly and tired, someone who needs a lot of care

   Emotions I associate with this word: fear, worry, needy

   Connotations (circle one): positive, (negative) neutral

   (Someone who is a weakling is not strong. Being a weakling is not an admirable trait.)

2. He was heavily armed—an air rifle in one hand, a wooden dagger in the other. (page 4)

   Images and experiences I picture when I read this word: soldiers, bank robbers, children playing a war game outside

   Emotions I associate with this word: fear, amusement, caution, aggression

   Connotations (circle one): positive, (negative) neutral

   (Someone who is "heavily armed" is considered a threat and dangerous. Because Avery is armed only with toy weapons, this description of him is also funny. The negative connotation of "heavily armed" is what creates the humor.)

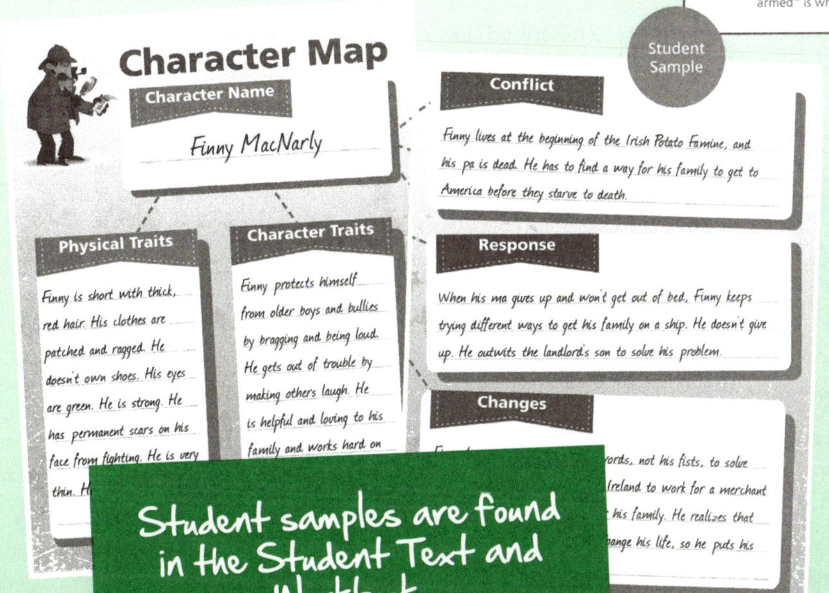

Student samples are found in the Student Text and Workbook.

The Answer Key does not provide suggested answers for unit projects and other open-ended assignments. In most of those instances, you will find a student sample in the Student Text and Workbook that can guide your feedback and evaluation of the student's work.

Readers in Residence TAKES THE MYSTERY OUT OF EVALUATING Your Kids' Work!

Rubrics

Use the rubric at the beginning of each unit in the Student Text and Workbook to direct your child's attention to the requirements of each unit project.

A rubric is a special checklist for evaluating and grading writing or other projects.

Rubrics for both the student and reviewers are specifically designed to match each unit's project.

The student rubric for each unit appears in the introduction and again in the last module of the unit in the Student Text and Workbook. Student rubrics are reproduced for your reference on pages 182–187 of this Answer Key.

The student rubric helps students learn how to evaluate their own efforts and track their progress. A reviewer's version of each rubric is provided in the appendix of the Student Text and Workbook. Parents, teachers, and other readers can use this rubric to give the student feedback on each completed unit project. (Students earn the average points of their score and the score from one reviewer, which they record on the Sleuth's Log in the appendix.)

Rubric for Unit 1 Project

Traits of Good Character Development	Points Earned
Physical Traits • I have described some of my main character's physical traits.	4
Character Traits • I have described how I will show what my character is like through what he or she says.	3
• I have described how I will show what my character is like through what he or she does.	3
• I have described how I will show what my character is like through what others say about him or her.	3

Rubric for Unit 1 Project	
Traits of Good Character Development	Points Earned
Conflict • I have described a significant problem my character faces in the story.	3
Response • I have described how my character responds to the significant problem he or she faces.	4
Changes • I have described how my character changes because of the significant problem he or she faces.	5
• I have described how I will show this change through what my character learns, says, does, or thinks.	2
Quality • I have created a complete project with the required elements.	4
• I have created a high-quality project. I was careful, thoughtful, and creative.	3
Effort • I worked hard on my project, and it reflects an appropriate amount of effort.	5
Conventions • I have followed the rules for capitalization and punctuation.	5
• I have checked to make sure all my words are spelled correctly.	4
Total	48

Unit 1 project: 65 points possible

Rubric Point System:

5 points – This part of the project is outstanding.

4 points – This part of the project is very strong.

3 points – This part of the project shows a lot of effort.

2 points – This part of the project needs improvement.

1 point – This part of the project is missing.

Scoring

The five-point rubric scoring system emphasizes "progress, not perfection" as the goal.

Students may fill in their average points on the Sleuth's Log in the appendix of the Student Text and Workbook.

Checklists

Use the checklist at the end of each module in the Student Text and Workbook to direct your child's attention to every task that must be completed in the module.

Checklist for Module 6

Directions: When you have completed a task, make a ✔ in the "Done" column. Ask a parent, teacher, or reading coach to award you points for each task using the checklist point system. Fill in the points you have earned on the SLEUTH'S LOG in the appendix.

Checklist Point System:

1–6 points may be awarded by a parent, teacher, or reading coach for each task completed. Here are the recommended guidelines:

6 – exemplary in quality *and* effort

5 – exemplary in either quality *or* effort

4 – acceptable in quality *and* effort

3 – acceptable in either quality *or* effort

2 – needs improvement in quality *and* effort

1 – incomplete

Tasks	Done ✔	Points Earned
6.1 Introduction to Animal Fantasy • Discuss the unique features of an animal fantasy book with a parent, teacher, or reading coach.		
6.2 The Parts of *Charlotte's Web* • Answer the questions based on your examination of the book.		
6.3 Make a Prediction • Answer the questions based on the information you collect from the table of contents.		
6.4 Read Kate DiCamillo's Foreword • Read the foreword by Kate DiCamillo.		
• Answer the questions on the lines provided.		
6.8 Read *Charlotte's Web*: Chapters I–III • Read chapters I–III of *CW*.		
• Fill in the CHARACTER INTRODUCTIONS chart with details about the characters.		
• Fill in the SETTING chart with details that show the time period and the place of the story.		
6.9 Ruminate: Chapters I–III • Ruminate on the questions about chapters I–III.		
• Discuss, draw, or write your answers to the questions.		
6.10 Aha! Chapters I–III • Answer the questions on the lines provided.		
• Refer to the chapters as you answer them.		

Student Copies

The checklist at the end of each module in the Student Text and Workbook helps students to stay on track and to complete all assignments.

Parent Copies

You will find the student checklists reproduced on pages 188–229 of this Answer Key. Use these checklists to track progress and evaluate student work.

Student Tasks

The checklist includes every task the student must complete in the module.

Scoring System

After students complete each assignment in the module, a parent, teacher, or reading coach should use the six-point scoring system to award points based on their effort and quality of work. Students may fill in the points they are awarded on the Sleuth's Log in the appendix of the Student Text and Workbook.

Guidelines for Evaluation

A guiding principle of the *Readers in Residence* series is "progress, not perfection." With this in mind, begin any evaluation of your child's work by considering his or her age and experience. Your feedback and the points you may award should always be based on a comparison of this work with your child's prior work. Use the point systems for both the rubrics and the checklists to set a standard for the student to reach toward.

Praise + Targeted Feedback = Progress

For maximum benefit, any evaluation of the student's work should be accompanied by targeted feedback. Targeted feedback is specific and concrete. For example, you might say, "Your answer to this question shows that you are thinking deeply about what you read. Can you list some details in the story that back up your answer?"

Praise—such as "This is excellent!" or "You've worked very hard, and I am so pleased"—is important, but this is not feedback. Praise is a source of encouragement—a gift we should give generously to our children. However, praise in the absence of targeted feedback doesn't help kids improve; it only helps them to keep putting forth effort. You will notice that the checklist point system is based on quality and effort. Parents, teachers, and reading coaches help students reach both of these goals with the powerful combination of praise and targeted feedback—and that produces progress.

Talk about It, Talk about It, Talk about It

So how should you proceed when a student's answer is wrong or wide of the mark? Simply talk about it—a lot. Ask questions, draw the student out, and try to get to the bottom of his or her erroneous thinking or lack of appropriate effort. Use the assignments in RIR as discussion starters. If students know you will devote time to talk with them as you evaluate the quality and effort of their work, they will put more time into the task in the first place. Where parents, teachers, and reading coaches commit their time shows students what is most important. So distribute your time wisely.

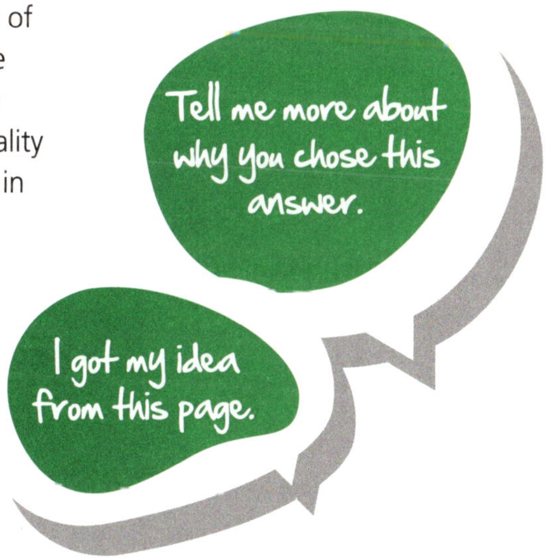

How to use the Student Text and Workbook

Welcome parents, teachers, and reading coaches! This introduction includes an overview of the teaching philosophy and methods used throughout the *Readers in Residence* series.

Why *Readers in Residence* Is Unique

Many programs help children learn to read. However, few teach students how to read to learn, and few cultivate heartfelt artistic appreciation. *Readers in Residence* is designed to do just that. We accomplish those goals in the following ways:

- providing detailed instruction in reading for inference
- showing students how to identify a text's genre and then deploy the reading strategies relevant to that genre
- teaching close reading techniques
- helping students to recognize and analyze the author's craftsmanship
- showing students how to use context clues to make educated guesses about the meanings of unknown words

The first step in reading comprehension is for students to identify the genre (or type) of text they are reading. While some reading strategies apply in all reading contexts, other reading strategies are required for specific genres. For example, how we read poetry is very different from how we read a newspaper article. Young readers need explicit instruction in these differences.

In volume 1, students are introduced to the following literary genres: historical fiction, animal fantasy, and contemporary realistic fiction. These are all types of narrative fiction.

Later volumes of the *Readers in Residence* series will introduce students to additional genres such as narrative nonfiction, historical nonfiction, scientific nonfiction, fantasy, speeches, editorials, poetry, news reports, essays, and more. By the end of this series, students will have mastered the elements of literature and have gained the reading skills necessary for a college prep high school course of study.

narrative fiction – Imaginative literature that tells a story with a beginning, a middle, and an end.

Who Should Use Volume 1

The target age group for volume 1 is fourth grade and up. The books selected for close study are written for a fourth through sixth grade reading level. However, they are outstanding stories of literary merit, so they appeal to all ages and are worthy of multiple readings. For this reason it is possible to use volume 1 with older students who struggle with reading comprehension or who are unfamiliar with the skills taught in this program. In units 2, 4, and 6, students complete a close reading of a book of their choice (from the genre specified). Older students can choose a book at a higher reading level for these units to make the program more academically appropriate for them. In addition, any of the activities in units 1, 3, and 5 can be eliminated or merely discussed with an older student. However, older students should read all of the instructional content to make sure they understand the skills and concepts that are integral to this series.

It is possible to use volume 1 with older students who struggle with reading comprehension or who are unfamiliar with the skills taught in this program. In units 2, 4, and 6, students complete a close reading of a book of their choice (from the genre specified).

How to Make RIR Work for Your Students

The *Readers in Residence* series is designed to be flexible. Please take advantage of this and set reasonable expectations for each student who uses the series. For elementary students, RIR is a challenging program, but not developmentally inappropriate. Challenge is good. Kids need to break a cognitive sweat if learning is to take place. They need a sense of accomplishment if we want them to take pride in their achievements. However, overchallenging children can be detrimental. They must feel successful, not frustrated. Because of age and developmental readiness, some students will complete volume 1 in a year; other students may need a year and a half. (Older students may complete it in just a few months.) It is important that students enjoy the process of learning to read critically and find pleasure in studying the assigned books.

critical reading – The process of analyzing how a text is constructed and interpreting what it means.

You can adapt the *Readers in Residence* series in several different ways to fit your family's overall needs and each child's readiness and interests:

1. As mentioned earlier, the books selected for close study in volume 1 are written for fourth through sixth grades. But you can use RIR with several different children at multiple grade levels at the same time. Be sure to adjust your expectations of each child accordingly. You can start the program with any student who is reading chapter books independently.

2. The program is thorough and systematic. It introduces new skills and concepts and gives students opportunities to practice using them. Exposure is the intention in the lower-level volumes; mastery is the goal in the upper-level ones. Lessons build on previously taught concepts and skills. Ideally, students should complete all the modules in a volume before moving on to the next volume, no matter what their age.

3. How a student completes that work is your choice. RIR includes a lot of questions. For a younger child, writing answers to all the questions may become a tedious chore. You don't have to require this! It's fine to just talk about some or all of the questions together. Just make sure the student responds to each question in some way. In many cases, discussing the comprehension questions with a student is the best way to help him or her grow as a reader.

4. If an assignment is too easy, it is fine to ask a student just to read through the material or modify the assignment to create greater challenge or interest.

5. The suggested schedule on pages xviii–xxii of the Student Text and Workbook shows 128 days of work. (The suggested schedule is also reproduced on pages 177–181 of this Answer Key.) This means that students can complete volume 1 in thirty-two weeks if they work on assignments four days a week. However, this is just one possibility. For continuity, most students should spend at least three days per week on this program. Younger students may find that spreading the work over five days per week for thirty-six or more weeks is the best plan for staying motivated and managing the challenge.

Co-ops, Reading Groups, and Reading Coaches

The *Readers in Residence* series works well with groups. The suggested daily schedule lists assignments for four days per week. The fifth day of any week can then be used for a co-op day or a reading group. In both of these settings, students can discuss their answers to the reading comprehension questions and share their progress on the unit projects with one another. Adult leaders can provide further instruction and feedback based on the material in RIR.

A reading coach is any adult who wants to guide students through the material in RIR in an organized way—through an online class, by individualized tutoring, or in a co-op setting. Additional materials for co-ops and reading coaches are in development. You can sign up to receive notifications about the release date for these materials and future volumes in the RIR series at www.readers-in-residence.com.

Teaching Philosophy

When I began homeschooling, I naively believed that teaching my children how to read was the end goal. Once that was accomplished, I thought they would then be set to learn independently. Even with my teaching background, I didn't understand that learning to read is just the first mile marker on the road to literacy. While learning to read puts our kids in the driver's seat on this journey, students still need continuing instruction if they are to reach the ultimate goal of reading for understanding.

RIR uses a teaching approach that is based on research. What do the most successful readers do while reading? How do developing readers learn these strategies? The answers to these questions were used to build this program.

Learning to read is just the first mile marker on the road to literacy.

Here are just a few of the critical skills expert readers deploy while reading:

- Expert readers form mental images as they read.
- Expert readers organize information as they read.
- Expert readers use their prior knowledge to increase their understanding.
- Expert readers ask questions.
- Expert readers make inferences.
- Expert readers determine the most important ideas or themes.
- Expert readers synthesize information.

literacy – The ability to use written and printed materials to improve one's knowledge and potential.

Notice in the list above that the responsibility is on the reader. What parents, teachers, and reading coaches can do is create a learning environment that supports the development of these critical reading skills. Here are the ideal conditions for emerging readers:

1. **Reading should be a pleasure.** Students should enjoy the books they read. However, many types of texts are an acquired taste. Students should be introduced to a wide variety of reading material and be shown how to appreciate their differences. As students gain greater understanding about the artistry involved in creating different types of literature, they will expand the range of books they choose to read.

2. **Reading should be a shared experience.** Writers need an audience. Readers need a community. Books connect us to other places and other lives—and they also connect those who share them with one another. What we read is kindling for our conversations. A complete reading program should include opportunities for students to talk about what they are reading with others who are reading the same books.

Books connect us to other places and other lives—and they also connect those who share them with one another. What we read is kindling for our conversations.

3. **Reading is an apprenticeship.** Children master the English language by deep and long exposure to writers who employ the creative potential of the written word for a wide variety of purposes. Students should learn to read closely and to notice what authors do to hold readers' interest, provoke their thinking, and focus their attention.

4. **Reading is an internal process.** A student's reading comprehension is largely invisible. RIR provides a variety of ways for students to demonstrate reading comprehension by including creative projects, thought-provoking questions, vocabulary work, and topics to discuss around the family dinner table. But reading comprehension is actually most developed by thinking deeply about what we read. That means students need time to read in an unhurried fashion and time to think about what they read. This is why students study only six books in depth in this volume of RIR. Students may not have the time to read all books s-l-o-w-l-y, but reading a few in this way will improve their pleasure and understanding of all the books they read.

Students need time to read in an unhurried fashion and time to think about what they read.

5. **Reading should be diverse.** Studies show that students who score high in reading on college entrance exams have been reading broadly for a long time. There is no shortcut to literacy. Students need access to all kinds of reading material—both fiction and nonfiction—and plenty of time to read. Homeschooling naturally affords students the kind of time they need. We just need to make sure we do not crowd this opportunity out of the school day. (If my own children were reading something worthwhile, I did not interrupt them to make them do something else.)

Teaching Method

General Overview

I understand the time constraints of parents and teachers. You are multitasking all the time—probably juggling many children, many subjects, and many schedules simultaneously. While this program is student-centered and student-directed, it is designed with parents, teachers, and reading coaches in mind as well.

In particular, the introduction, rubric, and checklists in each unit are designed to help you quickly grasp the assignments and your student's progress. This Answer Key is also written so that you do not have to page back through the modules to explain an answer. Even so, please preview *Readers in Residence* before your student begins this program. This will give you a better framework for understanding the teaching approach and activities. It will also show you the trajectory this volume follows to build students' understanding about reading and vocabulary.

The Role of a Parent, Teacher, or Reading Coach

The *Readers in Residence* series is designed for students to use independently, to the degree that is possible. Younger students and emerging readers need far more direct instruction and support from a parent, teacher, or reading coach than older, more experienced students. Greater independence will emerge as students gain greater control and mastery of the reading process.

However, the best reading experiences are often shared; therefore, one of the responsibilities and joys of a parent, teacher, or reading coach is to provide that community for the student. Without this camaraderie, assignments can become duties devoid of purpose. Join your child in this reading adventure by reading the assigned books as well. If you delight in the books you share with your children, they will see reading as an enjoyable adult activity, not merely a school assignment. Most of all, value the opportunity you have been given to share this process together.

Feedback

Targeted feedback is an essential support that parents, teachers, and reading coaches give to students. The rubric for each unit project is designed to help you do this. It lists the key components of the literary element the student is asked to focus on in that unit. Use the rubric as a basis for discussion and feedback. (See page 18 for a fuller discussion of the rubrics in RIR.)

What a child creates is a window into that child's intellectual life and development. Respond to a student's final projects as an interested audience. What aspects of the final project strike you as memorable or interesting? Talk about those first. What areas on the rubric seem underdeveloped or missing? Where would you like to know more? Approach sections in the projects that should be stronger with these types of questions. Celebrate effort, progress, invention, and careful attention to the elements listed on the rubric.

RIR frequently encourages students to talk through their ideas with a parent, teacher, or reading coach. These are points where adult support and input are necessary. Talking through the projects and critical reading questions, as well as helping students understand the most important elements to focus on in a reading assignment, will be essential to their success.

Talking through the projects and critical reading questions, as well as helping students understand the most important elements to focus on in a reading assignment, will be essential to their success.

Grading

I strongly recommend that you not assign letter grades to the assignments in this volume; rather evaluate each assignment for its strengths and weaknesses and for overall progress. The section on rubrics on page 18 explains how to use this form of assessment. Remember that exposure is the goal in this volume. I do not expect a fourth- or fifth-grade student to earn all the points available on most activities. Nor do I expect students to have solid answers to most of the reading comprehension questions in this volume.

How Books Are Selected

The assigned books used for close study in the *Readers in Residence* series are among the finest in children's literature, written by authors children should know. They also are exemplary for the element I focus on in each unit: character development, plot development, and setting. The three books assigned in this volume also consist of storylines that are age-appropriate for students in fourth through sixth grades.

Perhaps your children are already familiar with one or more of the assigned books used in this volume. Even if your family has already shared some of these titles together, much can be gleaned from rereading these books time and time again. In the same way that listening to a great symphony or viewing a famous painting many times increases our appreciation and understanding, rereading exceptional literature enriches our experience.

An On Your Own (OYO) unit follows the study of each assigned book. For these units students choose a book from the assigned genre. To assist you, a suggested reading list is provided at the beginning of these units. The reading list includes titles that fit the genre and the assignments in that unit.

An On Your Own (OYO) unit follows the study of each assigned book.

Like the assigned books, the titles on the suggested reading lists for the OYO units were selected because they are appropriate for the grade levels specified and will work well with the activities in that unit. The OYO reading lists include some books suitable for older students. My intention in providing the suggested reading lists at the beginning of the OYO units is to save parents time searching for a book to fit these units.

Other books not included on the suggested reading lists may better suit the needs of your family or the interests of a particular child. *Honey for a Child's Heart* by Gladys Hunt and *Read for the Heart: Whole Books for WholeHearted Families* by Sarah Clarkson may help you to find a suitable title that your child will enjoy.

Why We Have Chosen Specific Editions of the Assigned Books

Three notable children's books are assigned in this volume of the *Readers in Residence* series: *Sarah, Plain and Tall*; *Charlotte's Web*; and *Because of Winn-Dixie*. A specific edition of each of these books is recommended for three reasons:

- Students are frequently asked to refer to specific page numbers in these books to help them find answers to the reading comprehension questions.
- Having the correct edition will save you time when a student asks for your help.
- In this volume students will learn that important information can be included in the front and back matter of a book. For example, students are asked to read Kate DiCamillo's preface to *Charlotte's Web*. Only the 60th anniversary edition includes this information.

To help you find the correct edition, the ISBN for the assigned book is listed at the beginning of units 1, 3, and 5 and in the sidebar on this page.

The assigned books for volume 1

Sarah, Plain and Tall
by Patricia MacLachlan
(ISBN: 978-0-06-239952-6)

Charlotte's Web
by E. B. White
(ISBN: 978-0-06-440055-8, 60th Anniversary Edition)

Because of Winn-Dixie
by Kate DiCamillo
(ISBN: 978-0-7636-8086-2)

Repeated Elements

Unit Introduction

This page provides an overview of the unit for the student and the parent, teacher, or reading coach. It is designed as a reference tool to help you quickly grasp the assigned text, the genre to be studied, and the focus of instruction in the upcoming modules. A preview of the unit project is also provided, along with the rubric students will use to evaluate their completed project.

UNIT 1

Introduction

Sarah, Plain and Tall

by Patricia MacLachlan

Genre: Historical Fiction
Focus: Character Development
ISBN for page number reference: 978-0062399526

Have you ever ordered something special through the mail? Do you remember the anticipation of waiting for that special item to arrive? What do you think it would feel like to order a new mother by mail? Doesn't that sound strange? But that is exactly what happens in the first book we will study in this volume of the *Readers in Residence* series. Surprisingly, it is based on historical facts. A little more than a century ago, it was not uncommon for a farmer on the American frontier to propose marriage to a mail-order bride back East—a single woman who responded to an advertisement in the newspaper, indicating her willingness to consider such an arrangement.

Use the checklist at the end of each module to keep track of your progress.

5

Unit Project

Students are asked to complete a creative project after they finish each of the three assigned books. These creative projects are intended to be interesting and enjoyable for students. At the same time, the projects demonstrate how much students have learned about the element of literature studied in that unit. For example, after studying character development in the context of *Sarah, Plain and Tall*, students develop their own character. A preview of the project is included in the unit introduction.

Rubric

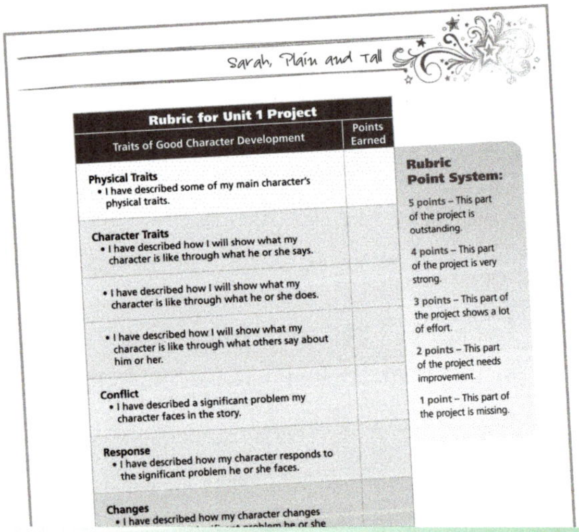
Sarah, Plain and Tall

Rubric for Unit 1 Project	
Traits of Good Character Development	Points Earned
Physical Traits • I have described some of my main character's physical traits.	
Character Traits • I have described how I will show what my character is like through what he or she says.	
• I have described how I will show what my character is like through what he or she does.	
• I have described how I will show what my character is like through what others say about him or her.	
Conflict • I have described a significant problem my character faces in the story.	
Response • I have described how my character responds to the significant problem he or she faces.	
Changes • I have described how my character changes	

Rubric Point System:
5 points – This part of the project is outstanding.
4 points – This part of the project is very strong.
3 points – This part of the project shows a lot of effort.
2 points – This part of the project needs improvement.
1 point – This part of the project is missing.

A rubric is a special checklist for evaluating and grading writing or other projects. The unit project focuses on the element of literature studied in the unit (e.g., character development, plot development, and setting). The rubric lists the characteristics that should be included in the final project. For most students, this will be their first introduction to the elements of literature, and the unit projects will be challenging. Keep this in mind when you evaluate the final outcome—celebrate your child's creativity and understanding. Progress, not perfection, is always the goal. Students evaluate their finished assignments with the rubric. Parents, teachers, and other readers use a reviewer's version of the rubric, provided in the appendix of the Student Text and Workbook. Students average the scores they receive on their own rubric and the Reviewer's Rubric, and they then fill in the average points earned on the Sleuth's Log in the appendix of the Student Text and Workbook.

Progress, not perfection, is always the goal. Students evaluate their finished assignments with the rubric.

Reader's Questions

At the beginning of each module, the Reader's Questions remind students to turn on their brains and get ready to learn. Students should hold these questions in mind as they work through the module to gain experience and expertise. At the end of each module, students will discuss their answers to these questions with a parent, teacher, or reading coach. This activity will reinforce their understanding and retention of the most important information in that module.

Reader's Questions
What is an expert reader?
What clues should I gather before I begin to read a book?
What are the characteristics of a historical fiction book?

Sneak Peek

This section at the beginning of each module provides a preview of the primary reading strategies and concepts that will be introduced in the module. These objectives also provide insight into possible answers to the reader's questions.

Sneak Peek

In this module you will learn:

- Expert readers study a book's cover before they begin to read.
- Expert readers identify a book's genre before they begin to read.

Student Samples

Samples of student work show students how to complete the module activities. Research indicates that when teachers provide examples of exemplary student work, student performance improves. For this reason, I've incorporated models and examples throughout this series. These student samples reflect the quality and effort expected for each assignment. Of course, you are encouraged to set appropriate standards for your children.

The Characters as I Imagine Them: Character Traits

Character	What I Think the Character Is Like	Details in the Story That Make Me Think This	My Prior Knowledge That Makes Me Think This
Anna	She is mature.	She does the baking. She looks after Caleb.	She has to take her mother's place. This responsibility makes her seem older than her age.

Student Sample

Reader's Toolbox

Throughout RIR, specific strategies that expert readers use are set apart in the Reader's Toolbox. The appendix includes a list of these strategies in an attractive, reproducible form for posting in the student's work area.

Graphic Organizers

RIR uses graphic organizers to help students generate ideas and organize their content. Graphic organizers are more powerful teaching tools than formal outlining because they help students visualize their projects and identify relationships.

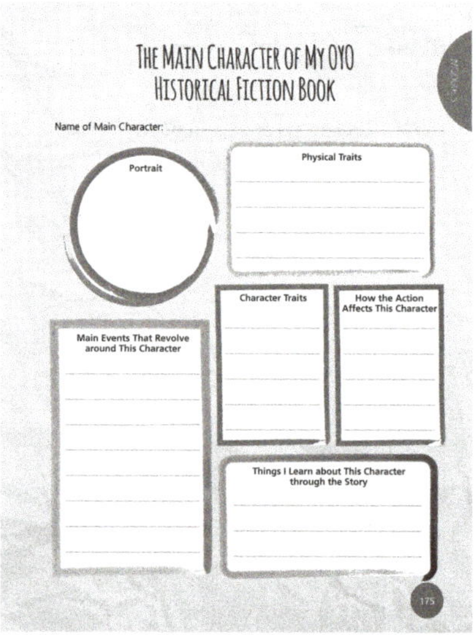

Reading Assignments

The reading assignments for each of the assigned books (*Sarah, Plain and Tall*; *Charlotte's Web*; and *Because of Winn-Dixie*) are listed in the Read sections of each module. These sections include the reading assignment and a focus for students to think about while reading. These sections often include a short activity to solidify students' understanding of the assignment.

Ruminate

The Ruminate sections are intended to help students think more deeply about the text and to make connections between the events in the story and their own lives. Students are given a number of options for how they respond to the Ruminate questions. They can use the questions as a discussion starter with their family, they can draw a picture that reflects their thoughts, or they can answer the questions in a reading response journal.

A reading response journal can be as simple as a three-ring notebook or as unique as a beautifully bound journal purchased at a bookstore. No matter what form the reading response journal takes, this is a place for students to record their reactions to the thought-provoking questions posed in the Ruminate sections. It can also be expanded into journaling about any of the books students are reading. The overall purpose is to create a keepsake that traces the influence good books have on a reader's life.

Encourage students to choose the option that they find most appealing or that best demonstrates their thoughtful answers to these questions. The most important aspect of the Ruminate section is the opportunity these questions give parent and child to connect these stories to their own lives and to each other. I hope the Ruminate sections add to the fond memories of your homeschooling years that you and your child are creating together.

Aha!

The sections labeled Aha! provide reading comprehension questions that measure one of two things. Some questions are designed to make sure students grasp the basic events of the assigned chapters. Other questions are designed to help students make accurate inferences about the events in the story. Students do not have to write answers to all these questions if they find this process tedious, but they should answer all the questions—even if they answer in the context of discussing their answers with a parent, teacher, or reading coach. Learning to read for inference is primarily accomplished in the RIR series through the Aha! reading comprehension questions.

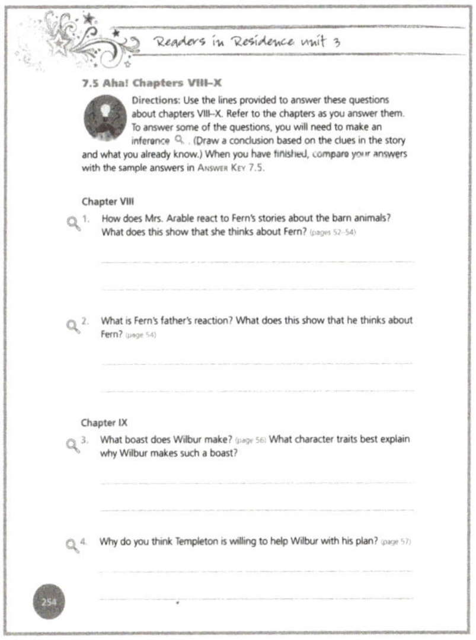

Readers in Residence unit 3

7.5 Aha! Chapters VIII–X

Directions: Use the lines provided to answer these questions about chapters VIII–X. Refer to the chapters as you answer them. To answer some of the questions, you will need to make an inference. (Draw a conclusion based on the clues in the story and what you already know.) When you have finished, compare your answers with the sample answers in Answer Key 7.5.

Chapter VIII

1. How does Mrs. Arable react to Fern's stories about the barn animals? What does this show that she thinks about Fern? (pages 52–54)
2. What is Fern's father's reaction? What does this show that he thinks about Fern? (page 54)

Chapter IX

3. What boast does Wilbur make? (page 56) What character traits best explain why Wilbur makes such a boast?
4. Why do you think Templeton is willing to help Wilbur with his plan? (page 57)

254

Especially at the lower levels of the RIR series, students will need adults to help them recognize the clues that expert readers use to make accurate inferences. You can use this Answer Key not just to check the accuracy of their responses, but also as a resource to help you guide them—like a classroom teacher working through the first exercise with students. The suggested answers can serve as a discussion guide to help point students in the right direction, to increase the depth of their understanding, or to show them a fuller range of possible answers to consider.

The magnifying glass 🔍 is used to indicate that students will have to make an inference in order to answer the question. An inference is a conclusion or opinion based on collected evidence combined with what is already known.

Word Sleuth

The best way to build a robust vocabulary is to learn words in context. Most words in the English language have several shades of meaning and many contexts for use. Studying words merely through dictionary definitions isolates them from a meaningful context. This limits a student's ability to understand how a word might be used.

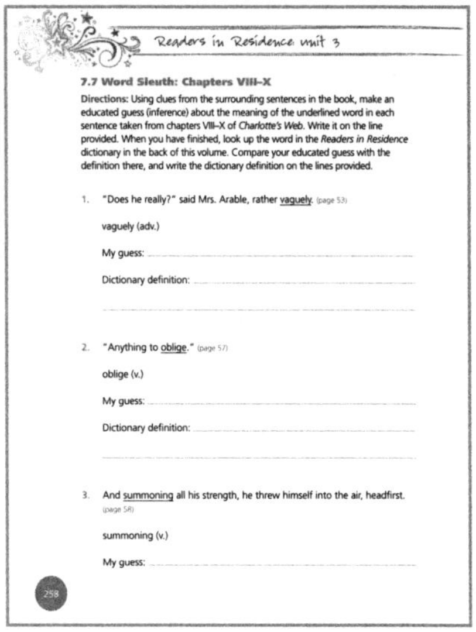

Readers in Residence unit 3

7.7 Word Sleuth: Chapters VIII–X

Directions: Using clues from the surrounding sentences in the book, make an educated guess (inference) about the meaning of the underlined word in each sentence taken from chapters VIII–X of *Charlotte's Web*. Write it on the line provided. When you have finished, look up the word in the *Readers in Residence* dictionary in the back of this volume. Compare your educated guess with the definition there, and write the dictionary definition on the lines provided.

1. "Does he really?" said Mrs. Arable, rather vaguely. (page 53)

   vaguely (adv.)

   My guess: ______

   Dictionary definition: ______

2. "Anything to oblige." (page 57)

   oblige (v.)

   My guess: ______

   Dictionary definition: ______

3. And summoning all his strength, he threw himself into the air, headfirst. (page 58)

   summoning (v.)

   My guess: ______

258

Vocabulary words have been carefully selected from each reading assignment. The Word Sleuth activities give students an opportunity to practice the process that expert readers use to decode the meanings of unfamiliar words. Expert readers gather clues from the surrounding context. (Interrupting the reading process to look up a word in a dictionary is a rare strategy.) Many of the words selected may already be familiar to some students. However, the words selected may be used in a new way or may add connotative value to the overall meaning of the passage.

RIR asks students to first make an educated guess about the meaning of the word from the surrounding context. The word entry also includes the part of speech that corresponds with how the word is used in the sentence. This is an important clue that students should use to help them infer the meaning. Then students are instructed to look up the definition in the RIR dictionary found in the appendix of the Student Text and Workbook and compare their educated guess with the dictionary definition. The student's attempt to deduce the meaning from the context is far more important than recording the dictionary definition. Please encourage students not to skip this step.

Conventions

Occasionally students are asked to notice how authors use the conventions of the English language in the text (e.g., capitalization, punctuation). Then they are asked to infer the rule that they think the author is following in the situation. The primary intention is to show students examples of the conventions used in context. I do not expect students to learn the rules through this approach, so their answers may not always be accurate. Students should be commended for noticing the convention and for making a reasonable guess at the underlying rule.

Ideally, the Conventions sections should reinforce what students are learning through instruction about the rules of English elsewhere. The companion *Writers in Residence* series provides instruction about grammar, capitalization, punctuation, and usage. The *Readers in Residence* series provides instruction in reading comprehension and vocabulary. Each series is designed to complement and reinforce what students learn in the other.

Book Talk

This section of each module provides discussion questions that students can use to talk about books in general with their family and friends. As you can see, a goal of the *Readers in Residence* series is to extend the books kids read beyond the school curriculum and into family life, where they truly belong. What you talk about around your dinner table is what you value most. If you want to raise readers, then include the books you are each reading in your nightly discussions.

Sowing Seeds

This section is designed to give parents, teachers, and reading coaches an opportunity to make connections from books to biblical truth. Spiritual growth can happen through listening to sermons or praying together, but it can also happen through considering what we read in light of Scripture. Great authors write about meaningful topics that prompt us to think deeply about life and truth. When we explore these topics through the lens of God's Word, we have an extraordinary opportunity to grow. This is one more way I hope the *Readers in Residence* series will help you enrich your family relationships.

Module Checklist

A checklist at the end of each module serves a twofold purpose: It helps students keep track of their progress and gives parents, teachers, and reading coaches a quick way to make sure students have fully completed all the assigned work in each module. The point system is a method of evaluation that emphasizes progress rather than grading. The student checks off the work he or she has completed. The parent, teacher, or reading coach awards points based on the point system provided.

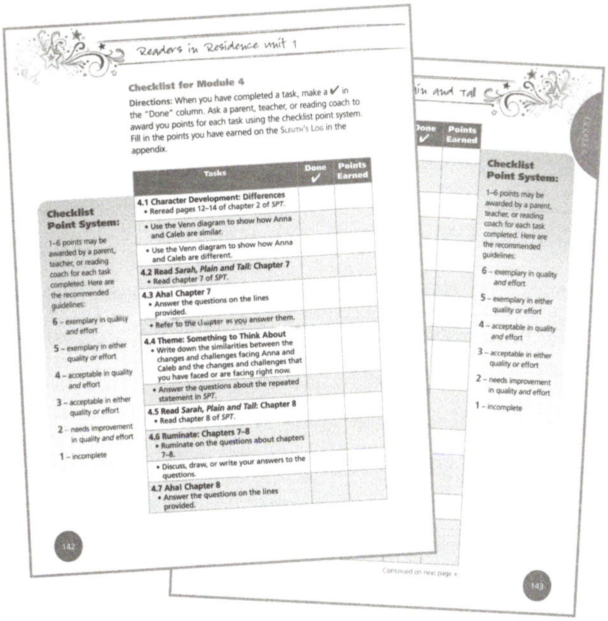

Readers in Residence unit 1

Checklist for Module 4

Directions: When you have completed a task, make a ✔ in the "Done" column. Ask a parent, teacher, or reading coach to award you points for each task using the checklist point system. Fill in the points you have earned on the Sleuth's Log in the appendix.

Tasks	Done ✔	Points Earned
4.1 Character Development: Differences • Reread pages 12–14 of chapter 2 of *SPT*.		
• Use the Venn diagram to show how Anna and Caleb are similar.		
• Use the Venn diagram to show how Anna and Caleb are different.		
4.2 Read *Sarah, Plain and Tall*: Chapter 7 • Read chapter 7 of *SPT*.		
4.3 Aha! Chapter 7 • Answer the questions on the lines provided.		
• Refer to the chapter as you answer them.		
4.4 Theme: Something to Think About • Write down the similarities between the changes and challenges facing Anna and Caleb and the changes and challenges that you have faced or are facing right now.		
• Answer the questions about the repeated statement in *SPT*.		
4.5 Read *Sarah, Plain and Tall*: Chapter 8 • Read chapter 8 of *SPT*.		
4.6 Ruminate: Chapters 7–8 • Ruminate on the questions about chapters 7–8.		
• Discuss, draw, or write your answers to the questions.		
4.7 Aha! Chapter 8 • Answer the questions on the lines provided.		

Checklist Point System:

1–6 points may be awarded by a parent, teacher, or reading coach for each task completed. Here are the recommended guidelines:

6 – exemplary in quality *and* effort
5 – exemplary in either quality *or* effort
4 – acceptable in quality *and* effort
3 – acceptable in either quality *or* effort
2 – needs improvement in quality *and* effort
1 – incomplete

142

Continued on next page »

143

Sleuth's Log

The Sleuth's Log in the appendix provides a place for students to fill in the total points they earn in the following sections of RIR:

- module checklists
- rubrics for the unit projects
- book clubs

Students can earn an award of distinction if they earn 85% of the points possible in volume 1. Submit your request to receive your award of distinction at www.readers-in-residence.com. You will find instructions on the home page.

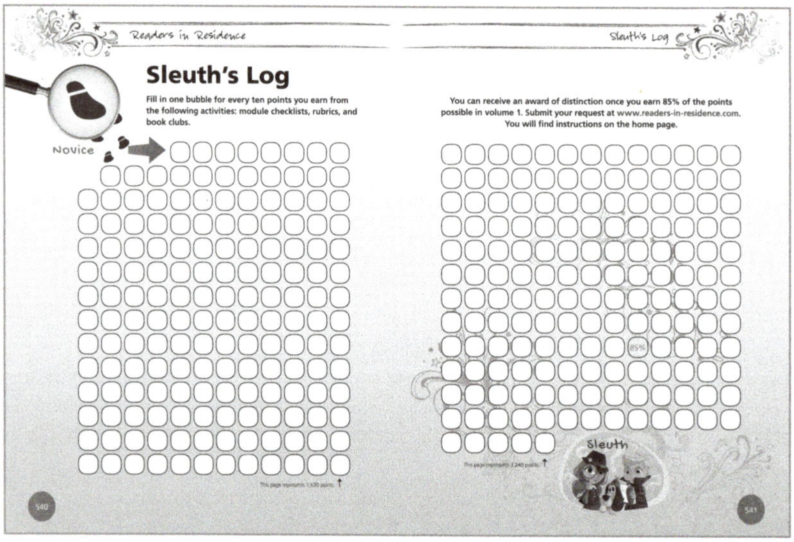

Book Clubs

To encourage your children to share the books they read with others, RIR includes a suggested book club for each of the assigned books. In addition, this volume opens with a kick-off book club and ends with a grand finale book club. These are intentionally simple so that getting together to talk about the books is easy to accomplish. The book clubs are likely to become a child's favorite part of *Readers in Residence*—I hope they are your favorite part as well. Sharing books with others has been a lifelong joy of mine, and I want to to pass on this delight. Writers need an audience; readers need a community. Add your own creative spice to the book clubs or simplify them down to the bare minimum. There are no rules you have to follow where the book clubs are concerned (other than just do them!).

On Your Own Units

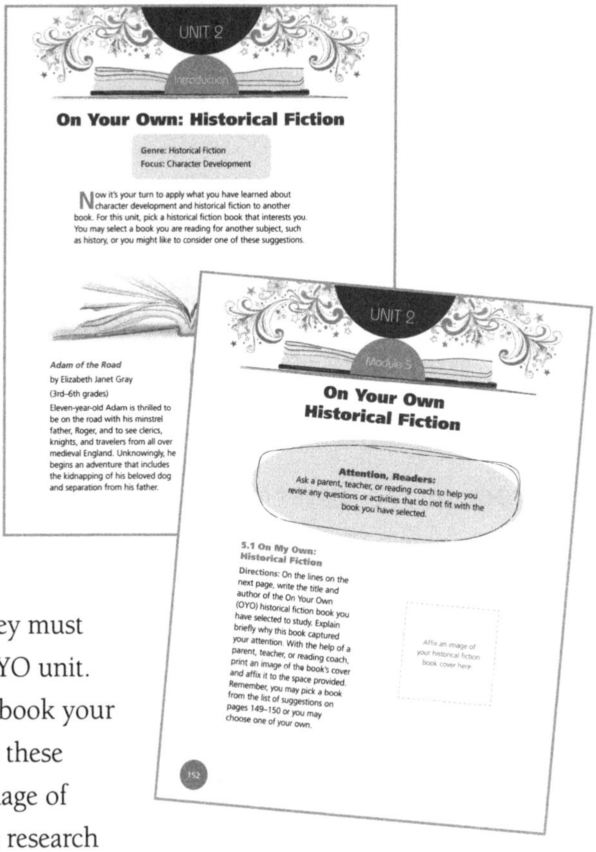
UNIT 2

Introduction

On Your Own: Historical Fiction

Genre: Historical Fiction
Focus: Character Development

Now it's your turn to apply what you have learned about character development and historical fiction to another book. For this unit, pick a historical fiction book that interests you. You may select a book you are reading for another subject, such as history, or you might like to consider one of these suggestions.

Adam of the Road
by Elizabeth Janet Gray
(3rd–6th grades)
Eleven-year-old Adam is thrilled to be on the road with his minstrel father, Roger, and to see clerics, knights, and travelers from all over medieval England. Unknowingly, he begins an adventure that includes the kidnapping of his beloved dog and separation from his father.

UNIT 2

Module 5

On Your Own Historical Fiction

Attention, Readers:
Ask a parent, teacher, or reading coach to help you revise any questions or activities that do not fit with the book you have selected.

5.1 On My Own: Historical Fiction

Directions: On the lines on the next page, write the title and author of the On Your Own (OYO) historical fiction book you have selected to study. Explain briefly why this book captured your attention. With the help of a parent, teacher, or reading coach, print an image of the book's cover and affix it to the space provided. Remember, you may pick a book from the list of suggestions on pages 149–150 or you may choose one of your own.

Affix an image of your historical fiction book cover here

152

An On Your Own (OYO) unit follows each of the assigned book units. Each OYO unit gives students the opportunity to apply the skills they have learned in the preceding unit to a book of their choice. Students may choose a book they are reading for pleasure or for another school subject. They can also select from the suggested reading list. The books on the selected reading list have been vetted to make sure they fit the assignments in this unit well.

The only requirement is that students must choose a book that fits the specified genre. For example, after reading *Sarah, Plain and Tall*, which introduces students to the genre of historical fiction, they must select another historical fiction book to study for the OYO unit. Even so, some of the activities may not perfectly fit the book your child is studying. Please feel free to modify or eliminate these activities. For instance, students are asked to find an image of the author of their OYO book on the Internet as well as research a few things about the author's life. If little can be found about the author or no image is available, then students can skip this activity, or you might ask them to research another author who writes in this genre. The important thing is that students have the opportunity to apply the skills and strategies they learned in the previous unit to another book.

Unit 1

Note: The answers to the questions in this unit are based on the following edition of *Sarah, Plain and Tall*: ISBN 978-0-06-239952-6.

MODULE 1

1.9 The Cover of *Sarah, Plain and Tall*

Directions: Answer the questions by using the clues you find on the front and back covers of *Sarah, Plain and Tall*.

These are sample answers that cover a range of things students may notice. It is acceptable for student answers to be shorter or less complete.

1. Who is the author of this book?

   Patricia MacLachlan

2. What can you find out about the author's life from examining the book?

   Answers will vary. Examples of details that can be found from examining the book are listed.

   Patricia MacLachlan is a Newbery Medal-winning author.

   She has written many other books for young readers. Some of these include *Caleb's Story*, *Grandfather's Dance*, and *The Truth of Me.*

   She has also written many picture books.

   She lives in Williamsburg, Massachusetts, with her husband and two dogs.

3. Who is the publisher of this book?

   HarperCollins

4. Why do you think the author decided to call this book *Sarah, Plain and Tall*?

   Answers will vary. Sample answers are provided.

   She wanted to tell readers who the story will be about. She wanted to name the most important character in the book.

5. Study the illustration on the front cover. What can you tell about the people in the illustration?

   Answers will vary. Sample answers are provided.

   The story takes place on a farm in an earlier time period. The family consists of a young woman, an older daughter, and a younger son. The flat field suggests a place in the Midwest. The family looks happy. The woman is collecting wildflowers.

6. What are the names of some of the characters you will meet inside?

   The following characters in the story are mentioned on the back cover: Caleb, Papa, Sarah Elisabeth Wheaton, and Anna.

7. What are some of the things you think you will learn about as you read *Sarah, Plain and Tall*?

   Answers will vary. Sample answers are provided.

   I think I will learn about the hard work involved in living on a farm. I think I will learn about the children's mother who died. I think I will learn about life on the prairie. I think I will find out if Sarah sings like their mother did. I think I will learn what happens when Sarah comes for a month. I think I will find out if Sarah decides to become Papa's wife.

8. How do you think the lives of the characters in this book will be different from your life?

   Answers will vary. Sample answers are provided.

   They can't travel very far because they don't have cars. They have to grow most of their food. They don't have cell phones or computers.

9. What do you think you might have in common with the characters?

   Answers will vary. Sample answers are provided.

   They probably have schoolwork. They have chores. They might like to play outside.

1.10 Clues to Genre

Directions: Write your best ideas for answers to these questions. Then talk about your answers with a parent, teacher, or reading coach.

1. How can the title of a book be a clue to the genre of the book?

   Answers will vary. Sample answers are provided.

   The title of a book can give you clues about when a story takes place. This can be a clue that the book is historical fiction. The title of a story can give you a clue that the book contains fairy tales or tall tales. The title of a book can let you know that the book is nonfiction because it is just the name of a topic.

2. How can the illustration on the front of a book help you guess the genre?

   Answers will vary. Sample answers are provided.

   The picture on the front can give you clues about where the story takes place. If the illustration contains a picture of a time long ago, this can be a clue that the book is historical fiction. If the illustration contains things that don't really exist, this can be a clue that the book is a fantasy. The pictures on the front can show you how the characters dress. This can also be a clue that the story took place in another time period or a fantasy world. If the illustration on the front is a photograph, this is a clue that the book may be nonfiction.

3. How can you figure out the genre of *Sarah, Plain and Tall* from the synopsis on the back?

   Answers will vary. Sample answers are provided.

   The synopsis tells me that the mother died after Caleb was born. This is something that usually doesn't happen today. Papa puts an ad in the paper asking for a wife. This is also something that doesn't happen today. He has to wait for Sarah to send a letter saying she will come and visit. Today someone would send an e-mail. Sarah also says in her letter that she will come from Maine to the prairie by train. This is not how people typically travel today. These clues tell me that the story is historical fiction.

MODULE 2

2.5 Read *Sarah, Plain and Tall*: Chapter 1

Directions: Read chapter 1 of *Sarah, Plain and Tall* by Patricia MacLachlan. Use the chart on the next page to list the characters you meet in chapter 1. Write some of the details you learn. Write how you learned each detail about the character using the list provided below.

Here are some ways authors reveal characters:

1. the character's words
2. the character's actions
3. the character's thoughts
4. the narrator's or another character's words or thoughts about the character

Answers will vary. Sample answers are provided.

Introduction of the Characters in *Sarah, Plain and Tall*

Character	What I Learned	How I Learned It
Caleb	He asks a lot of questions.	Caleb asks Anna questions in this chapter.
	His mother named him Caleb.	Caleb says this to Anna.
	He is younger than Anna.	Anna remembers when he was born.
	His mother died when he was born.	Anna tells the reader this. She is the narrator.

Introduction of the Characters in *Sarah, Plain and Tall*		
Character	**What I Learned**	**How I Learned It**
Caleb	His misses his mother.	Caleb asks lots of questions about her. He wants to hear about the day he was born over and over again. He likes the part where his mother said he was beautiful.
	He notices that Papa has changed.	Caleb asks Papa why he doesn't sing anymore.
	He wants a new mother.	Caleb smiles after Papa reads Sarah's letter.
Anna	She must be older than Caleb.	She can remember the day their mother died, but Caleb cannot.
	She feels impatient with Caleb for asking questions about their mother, who has died.	She says she has answered his question about Mama for the hundredth time that year.
	She acts like a mother to Caleb.	She warns him to stand farther back from the fire.
	She has a sense of humor.	She tells Caleb he looked like the lump of dough when he was born. She teases Caleb about naming him Troublesome.
	She does the chores that a mother would do.	She is making bread while she is talking to Caleb. She stirs and serves the stew.
	She hides things from Caleb that might hurt him.	She doesn't tell Caleb that their mother died because of his birth. She doesn't tell Caleb what she really thought of him when he was born. She hides her sadness from Caleb.
	She doesn't talk about her feelings much.	She does not share her thoughts about how she felt the day of her mother's death and how she feels when she looks outside at the prairie now.
	Anna wants a mother too.	Anna smiles at Caleb after Papa reads Sarah's letter aloud.

Introduction of the Characters in *Sarah, Plain and Tall*		
Character	**What I Learned**	**How I Learned It**
Papa	He is warm and affectionate.	He gives Anna a big hug when he comes in from the fields. Caleb runs to Papa and throws his arms around his neck. He says Jack, his horse, was feisty in town, but Anna tells us that no matter what Jack does, Papa loves him. He strokes the dog while he talks to Caleb and Anna.
	He is sad or lonely.	Caleb asks Papa why he doesn't sing anymore.
	He takes action to solve a problem.	Papa tells Caleb and Sarah that he has advertised for a wife in the paper because the children need a mother and he needs help on the farm.
Sarah	She has never been married. She loves the sea. She is not mild-mannered. She has a cat.	These are some of the details Sarah reveals about herself in her letter to Papa.

2.7 Aha! Chapter 1

Directions: Use the lines provided to answer these questions about chapter 1 of *Sarah, Plain and Tall*. Refer to the chapter as you answer them. To answer some of the questions, you will need to make an inference. (Draw a conclusion based on the clues in the story and what you already know.)

1. What question does Caleb ask Anna all the time? (page 3)

   Caleb asks Anna if Mama sang every day.

2. How does Anna end the retelling of the night Caleb was born? (page 5) Why do you think this ending is important to Caleb? Make an inference.

   Answers will vary. Sample answers are provided.

   She tells Caleb that Mama said, "Isn't he beautiful?" Caleb probably wants to hear this part over and over because it assures him that his mother loved him. The story gives Caleb a connection to his mother.

3. How did Anna feel about Caleb when he was born? Include a sentence from the chapter that supports your answer. (page 5)

   Answers will vary. Sample answers are provided.

   Anna didn't feel any love for him. She was repulsed by how he looked. A sentence that supports this is "He was homely and plain, and he had a terrible holler and a horrid smell."

4. What regret does Anna have about the night her mother died? Make an inference. (page 5)

   Answers will vary. Sample answers are provided.

   Because she was thinking about how awful Caleb looked, she forgot to say goodnight to her mother. Her mother died the next day. She regrets that she didn't say something that showed her love for Mama.

5. What time of year is it? (pages 5–6)

   It is near the end of winter. Anna says this at the bottom of page 5. On page 6, she tells readers that "patches of snow and ice" are everywhere.

6. What does this passage mean: "And then the cousins and aunts and uncles had come and tried to fill up the house. But they couldn't"? Make an inference. (page 6)

   Answers will vary. Sample answers are provided.

Anna means that their relatives came and tried to do things they thought would make Papa and Anna forget that Mama has died. Or they tried to do things that Mama did so that Anna and Papa wouldn't feel the loss of her. But none of these things helped to make them less sad.

7. Why does Caleb want Anna to remember Mama's songs? (pages 6–7)

   He hopes that if Anna can describe Mama singing, then this might help him remember her too.

8. What reason does Papa give for not singing anymore? (page 8) Can you think of another reason why Papa doesn't sing anymore? Make an inference.

   Answers will vary. Sample answers are provided.

   Papa says he has forgotten the old songs. He probably doesn't sing anymore because he is still sad about the death of his wife.

9. Why does Papa put an advertisement in the newspaper? (page 9)

   He puts an ad in the paper because he needs a wife and a mother for Anna and Caleb.

10. Why does Anna want to ask Sarah if she sings? Make an inference. (page 11)

    Answers will vary. Sample answers are provided.

    Anna wants Papa to ask Sarah if she sings because this is something she misses about her mother. Anna also thinks that people sing when they are happy, and she wants Sarah to have a personality that is similar to her mother's.

2.8 Read *Sarah, Plain and Tall*: Chapter 2

Directions: Read chapter 2 of *Sarah, Plain and Tall*. What do you learn about Sarah from her letters? Use the chart on the next page to list what you learn and what you expect Sarah to be like when she arrives at the Wittings' home. We've provided the first clue for you.

Answers will vary. Sample answers are provided.

Clues in Sarah's Letters			
What I Learn about Sarah from Her Letter to Anna	**What I Expect Sarah to Be Like Based on Her Letter to Anna**	**What I Learn about Sarah from Her Letter to Caleb**	**What I Expect Sarah to Be Like Based on Her Letter to Caleb**
Sarah can braid hair, bake bread, and make stew.	She is capable.	She has a cat named Seal.	She likes animals.
She prefers to build and paint.	She may not enjoy the tasks women typically do.	She says that Seal likes dogs "most of the time."	She will be funny and likes to tease.
Her favorite colors are the colors of the sea.	She loves where she lives. She will miss her home.	She says that his house sounds lovely.	She will be kind and thoughtful. She wants to assure Caleb that she will make an effort to like her new home.
She has a brother named William who is a fisherman.	She admires him. She will miss him. She will talk about her family and home.	She can keep a fire going at night.	She is capable. She will know how to help around the house.
She has sent a book of sea birds.	She is thoughtful. She likes to give gifts. She wants Anna to know about her life.	She says that she doesn't think she snores because "Seal has never told" her.	She likes to tease. She sees the humor in things.

2.10 Aha! Chapter 2

Directions: Use the lines provided to answer these questions about chapter 2. Refer to the chapter as you answer them. To answer some of the questions, you will need to make an inference. (Draw a conclusion based on the clues in the story and what you already know.)

Answers will vary. Sample answers are provided.

1. Anna says Sarah's letters arrived "before the ice and snow had melted from the fields." Do you think Sarah wrote back quickly or took her time? Explain your answer. (page 12)

   I think Sarah responded to their letters very quickly because Anna says in chapter 1 that it is near the end of winter and patches of ice and snow are still on the fields. If the ice and snow still haven't melted, then not much time has passed.

2. Why does Caleb read Sarah's letters over and over? (pages 13 and 15)

   He reads the letters over and over because he hopes she will become his new mother. He wants to figure out what she will be like from studying what she says in the letters.

3. What feelings are revealed through the questions Anna and Caleb ask in this chapter?

   Anna and Caleb are both afraid that Sarah will not like them or where they live and that she will not want to stay.

4. What does it mean that Sarah has said she will come for a month's time "To see how it is. Just to see."? (pages 15–16)

   Sarah is willing to come for a month to see if she likes the Wittings and if she likes their life on the prairie. Then she will decide if she wants to stay permanently.

5. Why does Anna first set the table for four people and then put one place setting away? (page 16)

   Either Anna forgets that her mother will not be there for dinner, or she is already hoping that Sarah will become a member of their family. Anna is preoccupied with thoughts of Sarah's arrival.

6. What is the special message Sarah includes at the bottom of her letter to Papa for the children? (page 17) Why does this make Papa smile?

   Sarah says to tell them that she does sing. Papa smiles because he likes what Sarah has said. He knows her answer will make his children happy.

2.12 Word Sleuth: Chapters 1–2

Directions: Using clues from the surrounding sentences in the book, make an educated guess (inference) about the meaning of the underlined word in each sentence taken from chapters 1–2 of *Sarah, Plain and Tall*. Write it on the line provided. When you have finished, look up the word in the *Readers in Residence* dictionary in the back of this volume. Compare your educated guess with the definition there, and write the dictionary definition on the lines provided.

1. It was dusk, and the dogs lay beside him on the warm hearthstones. (page 3)

   dusk (n.)

   My guess: evening

   Dictionary definition: The partial darkness between daylight and evening.

2. It was dusk, and the dogs lay beside him on the warm hearthstones. (page 3)

   hearthstones (n.)

   Dictionary definition: Stones used in front of a fireplace to prevent the sparks from catching the floor on fire.

3. It made a hollow scraping sound on the hearthstones, and the dogs stirred. (page 4)

   hollow (adj.)

   Dictionary definition: Empty.

4. "And Jack was feisty." (page 7)

   feisty (adj.)

   Dictionary definition: Lively, full of energy.

5. He said it harshly. (page 8)

   harshly (adv.)

   Dictionary definition: Sharply, unkindly.

6. She was round and slow and shuffling. (page 9)

   shuffling (adj.)

   Dictionary definition: Walking without lifting up the feet.

7. "My choice, as you can see, is limited." (page 10)

   limited (adj.)

   Dictionary definition: Restricted, without many options.

8. "What if she thinks we are loud and pesky?" (page 13)

   pesky (adj.)

   Dictionary definition: Annoying.

2.13 Conventions: I Spy Capitalization

Directions: Study the use of capitalization in the following sections of the book. Can you make inferences about why some of these words are capitalized? Answer the questions below.

1. Study the front cover of your copy of the book. What are some words that are capitalized? Write them below.

   Newbery Medal; Patricia MacLachlan; *Sarah, Plain and Tall*; Anniversary Edition; Newbery Speech & More; and all the words on the image of the Newbery Medal.

2. Why do you think these words are capitalized?

   Answers will vary. Sample answers are provided.

   "Patricia MacLachlan" is capitalized because this is the name of a person. "Newbery Medal" is capitalized because this is a proper noun. It names a particular thing. The other words are capitalized because they are titles.

3. Study the back cover of your copy of the book. What are some of the words that are capitalized? Write them below.

   Did, Mama, Caleb, Anna, Every, Papa, Their, Then, Sarah Elisabeth Wheaton, Maine, She, I, Will, The New York Times, School Library Journal

4. Read aloud every word that is capitalized on page 3 of *Sarah, Plain and Tall*. Write them below.

   Did, Mama, Caleb, Every-single-day, He, It, Every-single-day, I, For, The, And, And, Papa, Yes, Papa, Don't, Caleb, You'll

5. On the lines below, write down at least three rules you think may explain why some of the words you read aloud on these pages are capitalized.

   Answers will vary. Here are all the rules that apply:

   The first word of a sentence is capitalized.

   Proper names are capitalized.

   The pronoun "I" is always capitalized.

6. Why do you think the word *troublesome* is capitalized on page 4? What rule may apply?

   Anna uses "Troublesome" as a nickname for Caleb. That makes it a proper name.

7. Why are the words *Tennessee* and *Maine* on page 10 capitalized? What rule do these words have in common?

   These are states. The names of states are capitalized.

8. Why do you think capitalizing the words you found in these sections of the book is helpful for readers? How might readers be confused if these words were not capitalized?

   Answers will vary. Sample answers are provided.

   Readers may not know where sentences begin. Readers may not know when the author is talking about a real person. Readers may not recognize that a word is a proper noun, which names a specific person, place, or thing.

MODULE 3

3.1 Making Inferences: Prior Knowledge

Students are directed to use this exercise to notice how their prior knowledge and experiences come into play while they read.

Directions:

1. Review chapters 1–2. Then describe what you think each character on the chart on the next two pages might look like. Include the articles of clothing you think they commonly wear. Write the details in the story that help you to make an educated guess about your answer. In the third column, write the prior knowledge that also helps you make an educated guess.

2. As you read chapters 3–6 while you work on this module, add to all the columns on the chart.

3. Draw a picture of your favorite character so far in the story in the space provided. Or you can find an image that looks like this character to glue in the space instead. Show the physical traits you imagine. Make sure the picture fits the time period of the story.

   Answers will vary. Sample answers are provided.

The Characters in My Mind: Physical Traits			
Character	**What I Think the Character Looks Like**	**Details in the Story That Make Me Think This**	**My Prior Knowledge That Makes Me Think This**
Anna Image will vary.	Anna looks like her brother and Papa. I think she is tall and thin.		I know that members of the same family resemble each other.
	She is fair and thin.	In chapter 4 Anna says she is fair and thin like Sarah.	
Caleb Image will vary.	He wears long sleeves and long pants.	He is sitting near the fire, so it must be cold outside.	
	He has suspenders.		I know that men wore suspenders to hold up their pants during this time period.
	He is shorter than Anna.	Because Anna is old enough to remember Caleb's birth, she must be at least several years older. Therefore, she is probably taller.	I know that older siblings are usually taller than younger siblings when they are both children. When they are grown up, the younger sibling might end up being taller.
	He has curly hair.	In chapter 4 Sarah cuts his curly hair and scatters the curls for the birds to use in their nests.	

The Characters in My Mind: Physical Traits

Character	What I Think the Character Looks Like	Details in the Story That Make Me Think This	My Prior Knowledge That Makes Me Think This
Papa Image will vary.	Papa is taller than Anna.	He puts his nose in her hair.	
	Papa is strong.	Caleb can hang on his neck and swing back and forth. He works in the fields.	People who use their bodies to work are usually strong.
	Papa wears overalls, a hat, and a long-sleeved shirt.		I have seen pictures of farmers from this time period. These are the types of clothing they wore.
	Papa usually wears suspenders.	When he gets ready to fetch Sarah from the train, the book says he wears a belt instead of suspenders.	
	His hair is long enough to comb.	He combs and slicks back his hair when he gets ready to meet Sarah.	
	He is thin.		People were usually thin during this time period because food had to be grown and prepared from scratch. Farmers especially had to work hard. It wasn't an easy life.
Sarah Image will vary.	Sarah is strong.	She says she is strong in her letter to Jacob.	
	She wears long dresses.		I know that women during this time period wore dresses like this.

The Characters in My Mind: Physical Traits			
Character	**What I Think the Character Looks Like**	**Details in the Story That Make Me Think This**	**My Prior Knowledge That Makes Me Think This**
Sarah	She wears bright colors.	She says she will wear a yellow bonnet when she arrives.	People who wear a brightly colored hat usually like to wear other brightly colored pieces of clothing.
	She is taller than most women.	She describes herself as tall in her letter.	
	She is not beautiful.	She says she is plain in her letter.	From how Sarah has described herself in all her letters, I can see that she speaks frankly.
	Her hair is long and brown.	Anna says that Sarah smoothed back her brown hair into a bun, so it must be long enough to do so. In chapter 4 Anna says that she brushes her long hair.	

3.2 Character Development: Physical Traits

Directions: Review what you have learned so far about Anna. Then answer these questions. Talk about your answers with a parent, teacher, or reading coach.

Answers will vary. Sample answers are provided.

1. How old do you think Anna is?

   I think Anna is twelve.

2. What details in chapters 1–2 help you to make an inference about Anna's age?

   Anna takes care of Caleb and does the cooking and cleaning. She doesn't say things that will hurt Caleb's feelings. She keeps things to herself. She had to be old enough to remember Caleb's birth. I think Caleb is probably six or seven now. So that is why I think she might be at least twelve when this story begins. That would mean she was between five and six when Caleb was born.

3. What do you know from experience that helps you to determine Anna's age?

   I know that older siblings usually tell younger siblings what to do. I know that you have to be older to prepare meals and bake bread. I know that you have to be at least four or five before you can remember something that happened earlier.

4. What misunderstandings would you have about the story if you made the wrong inference and thought that Anna was younger than Caleb?

   If Caleb were older, it would be odd that he asks her so many questions. It would be strange that Anna tells Caleb what to do. I would expect Caleb to ignore Anna's instructions or tell her not to boss him around.

3.4 Character Development: Character Traits

Directions: Answer the following questions. They refer to the chart on the previous page.

1. What character traits on the chart do you think best describe you?

   Answers will vary.

   Now let's figure out what traits to assign to the characters in this story. Study this example from chapter 1, page 3 and see what you can figure out about Caleb and Anna from what they say and do on the very first page of the book.

> "Did Mama sing every day?" asked Caleb. "Every-single-day?" He sat close to the fire, his chin in his hand. It was dusk, and the dogs lay beside him on the warm hearthstones.

BOOK EXCERPT

2. Consider that Caleb has his chin in his hand. When someone does this, what does it suggest?

Answers will vary. Sample answers are provided.

He is relaxed. He is thinking.

3. Consider that the dogs lay beside him. What does it mean if an animal is willing to be near someone?

Answers will vary. Sample answers are provided.

The animals are comfortable around him. They trust him.

4. What character traits on the chart do you think best describe Caleb? Use the clues in the book and your prior knowledge of young boys and dogs to help you decide.

Answers will vary. Sample answers are provided.

I think that Caleb is curious, lonely, serious, tireless, thoughtful, and kind.

Now look at Anna's reply:

BOOK EXCERPT

"Every-single-day," I told him for the second time this week. For the twentieth time this month. The hundredth time this year? And the past few years?

5. What character traits on the chart do you think best describe Anna?

Answers will vary. Sample answers are provided.

I think Anna is impatient, busy, attentive, and mature.

Finally, study their next exchange:

BOOK EXCERPT

"And did Papa sing, too?"

"Yes. Papa sang, too. Don't get so close, Caleb. You'll heat up."

6. What does this bit of dialogue show you about Papa before you even meet him?

   Answers will vary. Sample answers are provided.

   Papa used to sing. He used to be happier.

7. What does the last sentence tell you about Anna?

   Answers will vary. Sample answers are provided.

   It shows she is older because she is warning Caleb to be careful.

3.5 Read *Sarah, Plain and Tall*: Chapter 3

Directions: Read chapter 3 of *Sarah, Plain and Tall*. Look for new details about Anna, Caleb, Papa, and Sarah. Add the physical traits to THE CHARACTERS IN MY MIND: PHYSICAL TRAITS chart in **3.1** MAKING INFERENCES: PRIOR KNOWLEDGE. Use the chart on the next two pages to list each character's character traits. Include details from the book so far (chapters 1–3) and your prior knowledge. (You may use some of your answers from **2.5** and **2.8** if they apply.)

Answers will vary. Sample answers are provided.

The Characters as I Imagine Them: Character Traits

Character	What I Think the Character Is Like	Details in the Story That Make Me Think This	My Prior Knowledge That Makes Me Think This
Anna	She has a sense of humor.	She teases Caleb. She says she would have named him Troublesome.	I can tell she is teasing Caleb, even though it doesn't say this. My dad teases me this way too.
	She feels guilty.	She thought Caleb looked horrid when he was born, but she doesn't tell him this. She regrets that she didn't say good night to her mother the last night she was alive.	I know that a lot of times I feel guilty if I think bad thoughts about another person in my family. I know people can feel guilty about the last thing they say or don't say to someone who dies unexpectedly.

The Characters as I Imagine Them: Character Traits

Character	What I Think the Character Is Like	Details in the Story That Make Me Think This	My Prior Knowledge That Makes Me Think This
Anna	She is quiet.	She doesn't talk a lot. She keeps her thoughts to herself.	
	She worries a lot.	Even before Sarah arrives, Anna is worried that Sarah will miss the sea and not want to stay.	
Caleb	He is eager to please Sarah.	He asks Anna if his face is clean enough.	I know that people get washed up when they want to look their best for someone.
	He is anxious.	He holds Anna's hand while they wait for Sarah to arrive.	I know that children want to hold an older person's hand when they are afraid or unsure in a situation.
	He is lonely.	He asks lots of questions about Mama and about Sarah. Caleb is eager for Sarah to stay.	
	He is impatient.	He rolls a marble back and forth while waiting for Sarah. He wants to know when they will sing immediately after Sarah arrives.	I know that sometimes young children do the same thing over and over again when they are eager for time to pass.
Papa	He is affectionate and warm.	He teases and hugs.	
	He thinks this is an important occasion, and he is eager to impress Sarah.	He dresses carefully before he goes to meet her.	I know that people spend more time combing their hair and choosing their clothes on important occasions or when they want to impress someone.

The Characters as I Imagine Them: Character Traits			
Character	**What I Think the Character Is Like**	**Details in the Story That Make Me Think This**	**My Prior Knowledge That Makes Me Think This**
Papa	He is kind to his animals.	He talks affectionately about his horse Jack in the first chapter. He talks to Bess and Jack before he goes into town.	I know that people who talk to their animals and give them names usually treat them like they are a part of their family.
Sarah	She is a happy person.	She tells Jacob to tell the children she sings in her second letter to him.	I know that people tend to sing when they are happy.
	She is confident and strong-willed.	She tells him she is not mild-mannered in her letter. She disagrees with Papa right away about where Seal will sleep.	
	She is a hard worker.	Anna notices that her hands are calloused and rough.	I know that people who work with their hands develop calluses.
	She is thoughtful.	She has brought everyone gifts she thinks they will like from Maine. She takes Caleb and Anna's hands the moment she meets them.	I know these are things adults do to show children they care about them.
	She is uncertain.	She looks out at the plains and says they look a little like the sea. But Anna sees the look on her face, and Anna thinks she is lonely already.	I know that some people try to look for the positives in a new situation when they are not sure how they feel about it.

3.7 Read *Sarah, Plain and Tall*: Chapter 4

Directions: Read chapter 4 of *Sarah, Plain and Tall*. Don't forget to add any new details you learn about the characters' physical traits to the chart in **3.1 Making Inferences: Prior Knowledge.** Use the chart below to make a list of differences between Sarah's home in Maine and Sarah's new life on the prairie. You may include details from chapters 1–3 as well as chapter 4.

Answers will vary. Sample answers are provided.

Sarah's Home	
In Maine	**On the Prairie**
Sarah lives near the sea. There are seagulls and other seabirds. She can go out in a boat with her brother. She can see the colors of the sea.	Sarah lives on the prairies. She cannot see any water. She can see the farm fields that surround her.
Her house is tall with shingles that have been made gray by the salt from the sea.	The house is small. The rooms are small. There is a barn, a windmill, and a windbreak.
Sarah could collect seashells.	Sarah collects wildflowers that do not grow at home.
She has her family close by. She lives with her brother, and the three aunts visit often.	She doesn't know anyone except the Witting family.
There are seals.	There are sheep and other farm animals.

3.9 Aha! Chapters 3–4

Directions: Use the lines provided to answer these questions about chapters 3–4. Refer to the chapters as you answer them. To answer some of the questions, you will need to make an inference 🔍. (Draw a conclusion based on the clues in the story and what you already know.)

Chapter 3

Answers will vary. Sample answers are provided.

1. Why does Papa slick down his hair and dress in his best clothes to go fetch Sarah? (page 18)

   He wants to make a good first impression on Sarah because he is hoping she will choose to stay and become his wife.

2. How do you think Anna and Caleb are feeling while they wait for Sarah to arrive? What clues in the text help you to decide? (pages 19–21)

   They are uncertain and nervous about whether Sarah will want to stay. I know this because the book says, "Maybe. Maybe our new mother." Caleb and Anna do their chores without talking, and Caleb is worried about his face being clean enough but "not too clean." Anna says that Caleb is afraid, and he asks her if Sarah will like them.

3. How does Sarah respond to Jacob when he says, "The cat will be good in the barn"? What does this tell you about Sarah's personality?

   She says, "She will be good in the house, too." This tells me that she is not afraid to say what she thinks and stand up for her own opinion.

Chapter 4

4. Who loves Sarah first? What does this show us about Sarah? (page 25) Why does Anna use the word *first*?

   Answers will vary. Sample answers are provided.

   The dogs love Sarah first. This shows she is kind to the animals. Anna uses "first" to imply that the whole family will eventually love Sarah too.

5. How does each of the Witting family members respond to Sarah when she first arrives?

   Papa is quiet and shy around Sarah. Anna says she is too. Caleb follows her everywhere and talks to her all the time.

6. Caleb thinks Sarah will stay with his family. What does Sarah say or do that makes Caleb draw this conclusion? (page 26)

   She says they can display the dried flowers in the winter. Caleb thinks this means she will still be there in the winter. She says that later they can look for the bird's nests made of Caleb's curls. He thinks that when Sarah says "later," this means she will stay.

7. In this chapter, Anna spies Papa tossing pieces of his hair into the wind for the birds. Why do you think he is doing this? What does this show you about Papa? (page 29)

   Answers will vary. Sample answers are provided.

   Papa is tossing his hair into the wind because he is happy and he likes the way Sarah has brought change. This shows that Papa is hopeful about the future and his sadness is beginning to leave.

8. What does Anna think while looking at her reflection next to Sarah's in the mirror? Why is this important to the story? (page 30)

   Answers will vary. Sample answers are provided.

   Anna thinks she and Sarah look similar in the mirror. She thinks that she could be taken for Sarah's daughter. This scene shows that Sarah is fitting into Anna's life and that Anna will accept Sarah as her mother if Sarah decides to marry Papa.

9. How is Papa described during the singing time with Sarah? (page 30) How has he changed from the first chapter?

   Answers will vary. Sample answers are provided.

   Papa sings as if he had never stopped singing. He is hopeful about the future. His sadness is going away.

10. How do you think Sarah feels when she remembers touching a seal? (page 31) What clues help you decide?

   Answers will vary. Sample answers are provided.

   I think Sarah remembers how much she loved touching the seals. I think she misses her life by the sea. The way Sarah imitates the seals, the way she sighs and agrees with Caleb, and the way she starts to sing softly are clues to how Sarah is feeling.

3.10 Word Sleuth: Chapters 3–4

Directions: Using clues from the surrounding sentences in the book, make an educated guess (inference) about the meaning of the underlined word in each sentence taken from chapters 3–4 of *Sarah, Plain and Tall*. Write it on the line provided. When you have finished, look up the word in the *Readers in Residence* dictionary in the back of this volume. Compare your educated guess with the definition there, and write the dictionary definition on the lines provided.

1. He brushed his hair so slick and shiny that Caleb laughed. (page 18)

   slick (adj.)

   Dictionary definition: **Smooth, sleek.**

2. I watched a marsh hawk wheel down behind the barn. (page 20)

   wheel (v.)

   Dictionary definition: **To fly in a circular or curved direction.**

3. Nick began to bark, then Lottie, and the wagon clattered into the yard and stopped by the steps. (page 21)

   clattered (v.)

   Dictionary definition: **Rattled.**

4. Sarah brushed my hair and tied it up in back with a rose velvet ribbon she had brought from Maine. (page 29)

   velvet (adj.)

   Dictionary definition: **Made of velvet—a smooth, soft type of fabric.**

5. Sarah sang us a song we had never heard before as we sat on the porch, insects buzzing in the dark, the rustle of cows in the grasses. (page 30)

   rustle (n.)

   Dictionary definition: **Soft crackling sound.**

3.11 Conventions: What Is a Sentence?

Directions: In the list below, circle the groups of words that make sense and draw a line under the groups of words that do not.

1. nose her said rubbing clear papa bess
2. caleb stared at papa
3. yellow bloomed flowers fields with
4. my hands are clean
5. shirt pulled caleb on my
6. the dogs barked

Directions: Here are some questions for you to think about. Write your answers in the space provided. When you have finished, discuss your answers with a parent, teacher, or reading coach.

1. What makes a group of words a sentence? Write your thoughts below.

   Answers will vary. Sample answers are provided.

   A sentence expresses a complete thought.

2. How would you explain the difference between the groups of words you circled and the ones you underlined to a younger sibling or friend?

   Answers will vary. Sample answers are provided.

   The underlined groups of words do not make any sense. The circled words do.

3. Choose a group of words you circled on the list and rewrite it below with proper capitalization and punctuation.

   Caleb stared at Papa.

   My hands are clean.

   The dogs barked.

4. Try to read the opening of chapter 3 below aloud:

BOOK EXCERPT

sarah came in the spring she came through green grass fields that bloomed with indian paint brush red and orange and blue eyed grass papa got up early for the long days trip to the train and back he brushed his hair so slick and shiny that caleb laughed he wore a clean blue shirt and a belt instead of suspenders (page 18)

5. Correctly capitalize and punctuate the sentences above. You can use your book to help you. Then read it aloud again.

Sarah came in the spring. She came through green grass fields that bloomed with Indian paintbrush, red and orange, and blue-eyed grass.

Papa got up early for the long day's trip to the train and back. He brushed his hair so slick and shiny that Caleb laughed. He wore a clean blue shirt, and a belt instead of suspenders.

6. In your own words, explain why the capitalized words and punctuated sentences are easier to read and understand.

Answers will vary. Sample answers are provided.

The capitalized words tell me where new sentences begin. They also tell me what words are the names of characters. The punctuation tells me where sentences stop and where I should take a breath when reading.

Directions: Look at the groups of words you decided made sense on page 83. Can you find the subject, predicate, and main verb in each one? Write them on the lines below:

1. Subjects: Caleb, hands, dogs
2. Predicates: stared at Papa, are clean, barked
3. Verbs: stared, are, barked

3.12 Character Development: Changes and Challenges

Directions: Repeat this process for other major characters. Try to find more than one change or challenge for each character. Ask yourself what new events or new experiences is this character facing.

Answers will vary. Sample answers are provided.

1. What changes and challenges does Sarah face?

   Sarah's brother is getting married, so she thinks she should look for another place to live.

   Life on the prairie is very different from her life by the sea in Maine. She misses the sea and her family in Maine. She doesn't know anyone in her new life with the Wittings. She has never worked on a farm before. She has not been a mother before. She is learning how to be a part of the Witting family.

2. What changes and challenges does Anna face?

   Her mother has died, and Anna is responsible for the house and for Caleb. She is lonely. She has regrets about not saying goodbye to her mother.

3. What changes and challenges does Caleb face?

   Caleb has no memory of his mother. He doesn't know what it is like to have a mother. He would like a mother who loves him. He wants Sarah to like him.

3.15 Read *Sarah, Plain and Tall*: Chapters 5–6

Directions: Read chapters 5–6 of *Sarah, Plain and Tall*. As you read, think about how Sarah, Anna, and Caleb each face the changes and challenges you listed in 3.12 CHARACTER DEVELOPMENT: CHANGES AND CHALLENGES. After you finish the chapters, use the chart on the next page to list the additional changes and challenges they face, and how they each respond to each one in the story thus far. Include the evidence that shows you this.

Answers will vary. Sample answers are provided.

Changes and Challenges Reveal Characters

Character	Changes or Challenges	How the Character Responds	Evidence in the Book That Shows Me This
Anna	Sarah is finding things she enjoys about the farm.	Anna is growing less quiet.	Anna shares her first word with Sarah and Caleb. She asks Sarah what her first word was.
		Anna is starting to believe Sarah might stay.	She also notices along with Caleb that Sarah says "our dune."
Sarah	She is learning about life on the farm.	She finds things she enjoys about her new life.	The sheep make her smile. She lies down in the grass and sings. She draws pictures of her new home to send to her brother. She tells William in a letter that she enjoyed sliding down a dune made of hay.
	She learns that life on a farm can be difficult at times.	She is tender-hearted. She gets angry. She wants to be alone. She works hard to adapt to her new life.	She cries when a lamb dies. She shouts at the buzzards that try to eat the lamb. She sits alone after Jacob buries the lamb. She learns how to plow a field.

Changes and Challenges Reveal Characters			
Sarah	She is getting to know Anna and Caleb.	She tells them about her life in Maine. She asks the children a lot of questions. She finds new things for them to enjoy together.	She tells them about sand dunes. She asks them to tell her what winter is like. She teaches them to swim in the cow pond.
Caleb	He is getting to know Sarah.	He talks to her a lot. He is eager to try anything she suggests.	He tells her his first word and asks what hers was. He climbs the dune too. He lets her teach him how to swim.

3.17 Aha! Chapters 5–6

Directions: Use the lines provided to answer these questions about chapters 5–6. Refer to the chapters as you answer them. To answer some of the questions, you will need to make an inference. (Draw a conclusion based on the clues in the story and what you already know.)

Chapter 5

1. How does Sarah treat the sheep? Why might her view of the animals make being a farmer's wife difficult? (pages 32–33)

   Answers will vary. Sample answers are provided.

   She treats them like pets. She gives them names and plays with them. She may find it difficult when it comes time to butcher or sell the animals.

2. What new character traits do you see in Papa in this chapter? Include the details in the book that show more of Papa's personality.

   Answers will vary. Sample answers are provided.

   Papa can be playful. He says the hay pile is "our dune" and puts a ladder by it so Sarah can climb up and slide down. He even climbs up and slides down it too.

3. What does Sarah think about her drawing of the fields? (page 36)

   She thinks something is missing, and she says this to Caleb.

4. How does Sarah describe the evening's experience to her brother, William, in her letter? (page 36)

   She says that sliding down their dune of hay was almost as fine as sliding down their sand dunes by the sea.

Chapter 6

5. The opening line of chapter 6 reads, "The days grew longer." (page 37) Why are the days growing longer?

   The season is changing. Summer is coming. The sun is up for longer periods of time each day.

6. In chapter 6 Papa teaches Sarah how to plow the fields. (page 37) What do you think this might mean? Explain your answer.

   Answer will vary. Sample answers are provided.

   This might mean that Papa wants Sarah to know that plowing the fields is a chore she will have to help with if she decides to become his wife.

7. Sarah asks the children about winter in this chapter. Why do you think she wants to know more about wintertime? (page 38)

   Answers will vary. Sample answers are provided.

   She may already be thinking that she will be there in the winter. Or she may want to know how difficult winter is on the prairie as part of making her decision about staying.

8. What differences do you see between Caleb's answer to Sarah's questions about winter and Anna's answer? (pages 38–40) Why do you think Anna describes wintertime as she does?

   Answers will vary. Sample answers are provided.

   Caleb is telling Sarah all the parts of winter he thinks will impress her.

He talks about how cold it gets, the blizzards, and lots and lots of snow. Anna tells Sarah about the fun things they do in winter time. Anna doesn't want Sarah to be alarmed by the prospect of a difficult winter. She is concerned that this will be yet another reason for Sarah not to stay.

9. How does Sarah describe the sea? (pages 41-42) Use a sentence from the book to support your answer.

   Sarah makes the sea sound beautiful. She says the sea stretches for as far as you can see. "It gleams like the sun on glass." (pages 41–42)

10. Anna falls asleep and dreams "a perfect dream." (page 42) What do you think makes this dream perfect for Anna?

    Answers will vary. Sample answers are provided.

    She dreams that the fields gleam like the sun on glass and that Sarah is happy. Anna probably believes that if Sarah can be happy on the prairie then she will decide to stay.

3.18 Word Sleuth: Chapters 5–6

Directions: Using clues from the surrounding sentences in the book, make an educated guess (inference) about the meaning of the underlined word in each sentence taken from chapters 5–6 of *Sarah, Plain and Tall*. Write it on the line provided. When you have finished, look up the word in the *Readers in Residence* dictionary in the back of this volume. Compare your educated guess with the definition there, and write the dictionary definition on the lines provided.

1. She sank her fingers into their thick, coarse wool. (page 32)

   coarse (adj.)

   Dictionary definition: Not fine or smooth, rough.

2. She lay down in the field beside them and sang "Sumer Is Icumen in," her voice drifting over the meadow grasses, carried by the wind. (page 28)

drifting (v.)

Dictionary definition: **Carrying along by wind or water.**

3. "Dune," said Sarah. (page 33)

   dune (n.)

   Dictionary definition: **A hill or ridge of sand created by the wind.**

4. "It was soft and sparkling with bits of mica, and when we were little we would slide down the dune into the water." (pages 33–34)

   mica (n.)

   Dictionary definition: **A lustrous rock-forming mineral.**

5. Next to the barn was Papa's mound of hay for bedding, nearly half as tall as the barn, covered with canvas to keep the rain from rotting it. (page 34)

   canvas (n.)

   Dictionary definition: **Sturdy cloth made from hemp, flax, or cotton.**

6. Sarah and I watched him jump over rock and gullies, the sheep behind him, stiff legged and fast. (page 40)

   gullies (n.)

   Dictionary definition: **Ditches created by recurring rainwater.**

7. "Shoo, cows," said Sarah as the cows looked up, startled. (page 41)

   startled (v.)

   Dictionary definition: **Suddenly surprised.**

8. The fields had turned to a sea that gleamed like sun on glass. (page 42)

   gleamed (v.)

   Dictionary definition: **Sparkled, twinkled.**

3.19 Conventions: What Is a Paragraph?

Directions: Answer the questions about the paragraphs in chapter 5 of *Sarah, Plain and Tall*. You will need to use your book to answers these questions.

1. What is the topic of the second paragraph on page 32?

   The main topic of this paragraph is Sarah's reaction to the death of a lamb.

2. How is the topic of this paragraph different from the one before it and the one after it?

   The one before it is about how Sarah showed her love for the sheep. The one after it is about the pictures Sarah drew of her new life to send to her family back home in Maine.

3. Look at the rest of the paragraphs on pages 33–34. Can you figure out another rule of paragraphs that applies to the dialogue in a story? Write it below.

   Writers start a new paragraph every time the speaker in a section of dialogue changes.

4. How do the rules for paragraphs help readers to understand the story better?

   Paragraphs tell readers when the topic changes or the speaker changes.

MODULE 4

4.1 Character Development: Differences

Directions: Use the Venn diagram on the next page to compare and contrast Anna and Caleb. List all the ways you can think of that Anna and Caleb are similar to each other. Then list all the ways that they are different from each other.

Answers will vary. Sample answers are provided.

Compare and Contrast: Anna and Caleb

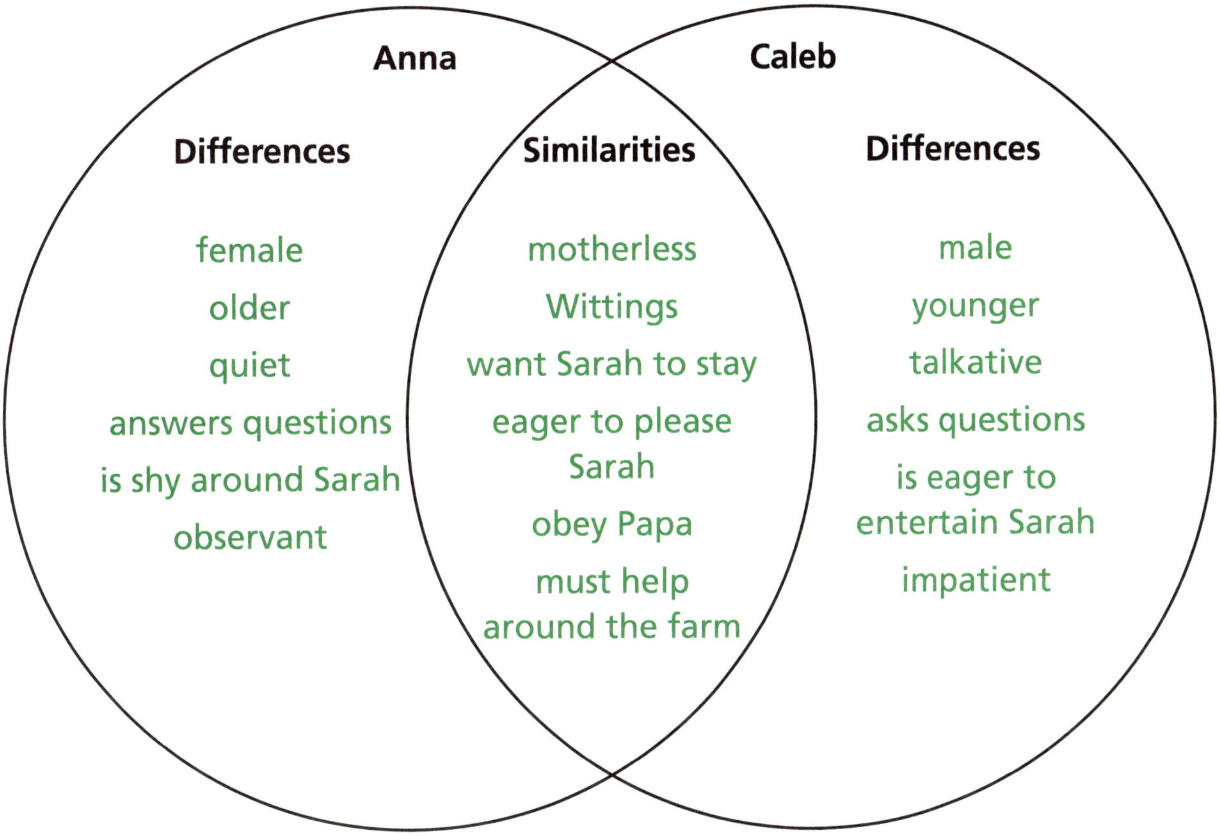

4.3 Aha! Chapter 7

Directions: Use the lines provided to answer these questions about chapter 7. Refer to the chapter as you answer them. To answer some of the questions, you will need to make an inference 🔍. (Draw a conclusion based on the clues in the story and what you already know.)

1. 🔍 What is the season of the year? Use a sentence from the book to support your answer.

   It is summer. "The summer roses were opening." (page 43)

2. Who is coming to the Witting farm and why are they coming? (page 43)

   Matthew and Maggie and their children have come. They've come to help Jacob plow a new field.

3. What gifts does Sarah receive from the neighbor? (pages 44, 46–47) Why do you think the neighbor gives these gifts?

Answers will vary. Sample answers are provided.

Sarah receives chickens and flowers for her garden. I think Maggie wants to be friends with Sarah. I think one gift is practical and the other is for Sarah to have something pretty to look at. Maggie knows what it is like to move to a new place. She may think that a garden will help the prairie feel like home for Sarah.

4. Maggie is previously mentioned in this story. (pages 9–10) Why does Papa talk about Maggie in chapter 1?

Maggie was also a mail-order bride.

5. Anna overhears a conversation between Maggie and Sarah. (pages 45–46) What does Maggie miss? What does Sarah miss?

Maggie misses the hills of Tennessee. Sarah says that she misses the sea, her brother William, and the aunts.

6. What is Anna's reaction to their conversation? (page 45) What does Anna admit to herself that she misses? (page 46)

She is upset and doesn't want the women to miss things from their former lives. Anna admits to herself that she misses Mama.

7. How does Maggie encourage Sarah? (page 46) Do you think this advice would encourage Anna too? Why?

Answers will vary. Sample answers are provided.

Maggie tells Sarah there are always things to miss no matter where you are. I think this advice will help Anna to understand that missing things is a normal part of life. Missing something we once had doesn't mean we want to leave where we are.

8. What do Anna and Sarah and Maggie plant? (page 47) What are some other times flowers have been mentioned in this story?

They plant zinnias, marigolds, and wild feverfew. Flowers are mentioned on the day Sarah arrives (page 18) and are placed in her room for her arrival (page 24). Sarah picks flowers to dry the day after she arrives (pages 26–27). Sarah has daisies in her hair that Papa has picked for her on the day of Matthew and Maggie's visit (pages 43–44).

9. Twice in this chapter, Papa gives Sarah flowers. Find two sentences to show this. What might this indicate?

   Answers will vary. Sample answers are provided.

   "Papa had picked them for her" (page 44). "And then Papa came, just before the rain, bringing Sarah the first roses of summer" (page 49). Papa is starting to fall in love with Sarah. Papa has noticed that Sarah likes flowers, and he wants to please her.

4.4 Theme: Something to Think About

Directions: Find the statement that is made twice in chapter 7 and answer the questions below. Talk about your answers with a parent, teacher, or reading coach.

1. Write the statement that sums up one of Patricia MacLachlan's themes.

   There is always something to miss, no matter where you are.

2. What do you think this statement means?

   Answers will vary. Sample answers are provided.

   This is good advice that helps both women to understand that even if they went back to their old life, they would then miss something or someone from where they are now.

3. List some things that you miss.

   Answers will vary.

4. How can this understanding help you face a change or challenge in the future?

   Answers will vary. Sample answers are provided.

   Change often means we must leave something or someone behind. This is just a normal part of growing up. If we understand that missing the things we once had is normal, it might make it easier to adjust to changes.

4.7 Aha! Chapter 8

Directions: Use the lines provided to answer these questions about chapter 8. Refer to the chapter as you answer them. To answer some of the questions, you will need to make an inference 🔍. (Draw a conclusion based on the clues in the story and what you already know.)

1. Throughout the book, the weather and the seasons provide clues to events in the story. At the beginning of chapter 8, we learn that "strange clouds hung in the northwest, low and black and green." (page 50) What might this mean to the Witting family? How does this make you feel?

   Answers will vary. Sample answers are provided.

   A storm is brewing, and they should get prepared. A storm can damage crops and their buildings. Animals can be lost or injured in a storm. The threat of bad weather can make readers feel a sense of foreboding.

2. Sarah shows herself to be different than other women the children have known. List some of her unique characteristics that you have noticed throughout the book.

   Answers will vary. Sample answers are provided.

   Sarah says she would rather build bookshelves and paint than cook. Sarah speaks her mind and tells Jacob she is not mild-mannered. She is able to repair a roof and wants to wear overalls.

3. Why doesn't Caleb want Sarah to learn to drive a wagon? (page 51) Do you think Anna feels the same way about this as Caleb? Explain your reasoning.

   Answers will vary. Sample answers are provided.

   He is afraid she will use it to drive herself to the train station so she can leave. Anna may have the same fear because she has tears in her eyes. Or she may know that if Sarah is going to leave, she will leave whether she can drive the wagon or not. Anna may realize how sad she will be if Sarah doesn't stay.

4. What is in Sarah's arms when she comes into the barn for the last time? (page 55) Do you think this is unusual? Did it take you by surprise? What might this mean?

Answers will vary. Sample answers are provided.

She is carrying summer roses. These are probably the roses Papa has given to her. It is unusual to think about saving flowers in a serious storm unless they are very important to you. This may mean that she is also starting to love Papa.

5. What question does Caleb ask Sarah after looking out the barn window during the storm for the last time? (page 55) How does Sarah answer? Why might this be important?

   Answers will vary. Sample answers are provided.

   Caleb asks what color the sea is when it storms. Sarah says it is blue and gray and green. Caleb has figured out what is missing from Sarah's drawing.

6. How does Sarah try to comfort Papa? (page 56) How is this moment different from most of the other moments in the story so far? What might this mean?

   Answers will vary. Sample answers are provided.

   Sarah tells Papa everything will be all right. She has been through similar squalls in Maine. Sarah is comforting Papa. She is giving him strength. They are growing closer.

7. What memory does Anna have when she sees Papa and Sarah standing together? (page 56)

   She remembers her mother and Papa standing together in the same way, only Mama was smaller than Sarah and had fair hair.

8. How is the hail on the ground described at the end of chapter 8? Why might this be important?

   Answers will vary. Sample answers are provided.

   "It was white and gleaming for as far as we looked like sun on glass. Like the sea." The colors of the sky during the storm and the hail on the ground afterward may remind Sarah of the sea. Perhaps she will come to love this place in the same way that she loved her home in Maine.

4.8 Character Development: Changes

Directions: Characters often change near the end of the book. Be alert for characters who learn something new, speak differently, act in a new or surprising way, or think differently about a challenge. Use the chart on the next page to write something new you notice about each character in chapters 7–8. You may have to reread these chapters to help you decide.

Answers will vary. Sample answers are provided. Students are asked to supply only one example of something new.

I Spy Something New	
Anna	Anna remembers standing on the porch with Caleb waiting with Sarah. Now they are standing on the porch with Sarah waiting for the neighbors. Anna admits to herself that she misses Mama. Anna shows that she knows Sarah better—she knows the chickens will not be for eating.
Sarah	Sarah is wearing her hair in braids entwined with flowers Papa has picked for her. She must be growing closer to Papa. Sarah has a new friend in Maggie who understands how she feels. Sarah puts on a pair of men's overalls. She goes to the barn to have an argument with Papa. Both of these are new. Sarah helps Papa to fix the roof before the storm.
Papa	Papa brings Sarah roses. He is clearly courting her. Papa is good at resolving the argument with Sarah. Papa shows that he is worried about the storm.

4.9 Read *Sarah, Plain and Tall*: Chapter 9

Directions: Read chapter 9 of *Sarah, Plain and Tall*. The climax of the story comes in this chapter. The climax is the point where readers feel the most tension because the major characters' main conflict comes to a head and is resolved. (You will learn more about the climax of a story in unit 3.) As you read chapter 9, notice how each character responds to Sarah's trip into town.

What Does Each Character Think, Say, and Do?	
Sarah	Sarah is excited. She gets up early, and she has on her best clothes. She kisses everyone goodbye. When she returns she says she will always miss the sea, but she would miss them more if she were to leave. Sarah brings the colors of the sea back home with her in the colored pencils.
Anna	Anna takes Caleb into the barn, where they both cry. After Sarah leaves, Anna thinks about the day people took Mama away in the wagon. She does her chores. Anna tries to assure Caleb that Sarah will come back because Seal is here, but she is still worried. She is afraid to ask Papa if Sarah is coming back.
Caleb	Caleb tries to think of things to do to keep her from going. He starts to cry. After Sarah leaves, Caleb holds Anna's hand. Caleb loudly lists all the reasons she will not come back.
Papa	Papa gives her lots of advice. He says it is very good after she leaves, and he goes back to work. Papa doesn't seem worried. He says Sarah is Sarah and she will do what she is going to do. He understands that he cannot do anything else to make her stay.

4.11 Aha! Chapter 9

Directions: Use the lines provided to answer these questions about chapter 9. Refer to the chapter as you answer them. To answer some of the questions, you will need to make an inference 🔍. (Draw a conclusion based on the clues in the story and what you already know.)

1. What promise does Papa keep to Sarah? (pages 59–60)

   He teaches her how to drive the wagon.

2. What ideas does Caleb have to keep Sarah from going into town? (page 59)

   He says that they could tie her up or he could get sick.

3. Why does Anna go into the barn after Caleb leaves to cut firewood? (page 60)

   She wants to be alone with her worries. She doesn't want anyone else to see how upset she is.

4. What does Sarah say to the children when she leaves in the wagon? (page 61)

   She tells them to take care of Seal.

5. Why does Anna remember the day her mother was taken away in the wagon on this day? (page 61)

   She is reminded of the day her mother is taken away because it was also a sunny day like this one. She remembers because she is afraid that Sarah will not come back.

6. What question does Anna ask Caleb about the picture? (page 62) Does this seem unusual to you?

   Anna asks him what he noticed was missing from the picture. It is unusual that Anna is asking a question and Caleb is the one with the answer.

7. What does Papa mean when he says, "Sarah is Sarah. She does things her way"? (page 63)

   Answers will vary. Sample answers are provided.

   Papa understands that Sarah has a mind of her own. He knows that it will be hard to predict what Sarah will do.

8. What inference can you make about Caleb when he tells Sarah that "Seal was very worried"? (page 64)

   Answers will vary. Sample answers are provided.

   This is Caleb's way of explaining his tears and hiding the fact that he was very worried.

9. What does Sarah bring back in her packages for Anna and Caleb? (pages 65–66) How might each gift reassure the children that Sarah is not planning to leave?

   Answers will vary. Sample answers are provided.

   Sarah brings colored pencils. This means they will be drawing pictures of their new life together on the prairies. It means she has thought of a way to capture what she misses while staying in her new home.

10. We read that Sarah brings home nasturtium seeds, candles, and a book of songs from her trip into town. (page 66) What do these items suggest to you about the future for the Witting family?

   Answers will vary. Sample answers are provided.

   Sarah is certainly staying. They are going to plant flowers together and sing. The Wittings will be a happy family.

4.12 Word Sleuth: Chapters 7–9

Directions: Using clues from the surrounding sentences in the book, make an educated guess (inference) about the meaning of the underlined word in each sentence taken from chapters 7–9 of *Sarah, Plain and Tall*. Write it on the line provided. When you have finished, look up the word in the *Readers in Residence* dictionary in the back of this volume. Compare your educated guess with the definition there, and write the dictionary definition on the lines provided.

1. Old Bess and Jack ran along the inside of the fence, whickering at the new horses. (page 44)

   whickering (v.)

   Dictionary definition: **Whinnying softly, neighing.**

2. They followed her, shuffling and scratching primly in the dirt. (page 44)

   primly (adv.)

   Dictionary definition: **Stiffly and properly.**

3. I have tansy. (page 48)

   tansy (n.)

   Dictionary definition: **A strong-scented, weedy herb.**

4. "This woman does," said Sarah crisply. (page 50)

   crisply (adv.)

   Dictionary definition: Sharply and concisely.

5. "Not Jack," he said. "Jack is sly." (page 51)

   sly (adj.)

   Dictionary definition: Mischievous, sneaky.

6. "A squall!" he yelled to us. (page 53)

   squall (n.)

   Dictionary definition: Sudden, violent windstorm accompanied by rain or snow.

7. There was a hiss of wind, a sudden pungent smell. (page 53)

   pungent (adj.)

   Dictionary definition: Sharp, acrid taste or smell.

8. The sheep nosed open their stall door and milled around the barn, bleating. (page 54)

   milled (v.)

   Dictionary definition: Moved around in a confused or aimless way.

9. I went into the safe darkness of the barn then, Sarah's chickens scuttling along behind me. (page 60)

   scuttling (v.)

   Dictionary definition: Scurrying.

10. Very carefully, I unwrapped it, Caleb peering closely. (pages 65–66)

   peering (v.)

   Dictionary definition: Looking intently.

4.13 Conventions: What Is a Chapter?

Directions: In the last module you studied two organizational units that writers use: the sentence and the paragraph. Now think about the next level authors use to organize their ideas in a book: the chapter. Answer the questions with your best ideas.

Answers will vary. Sample answers are provided.

1. Why do you think most authors divide their books into chapters? How does this convention make it easier for the reader to understand the story?

   Authors use chapters to show the beginning and end of the main events in a story. This helps readers to expect that a new event or a new time period may begin in the next chapter.

2. Read the first and last paragraph of every chapter in *Sarah, Plain and Tall*. Explain in your own words why you think Patricia MacLachlan decided to divide her story into these chapters. Discuss your ideas with a parent, teacher, or reading coach.

   The opening and closing lines of each chapter show the beginning and ending of an episode in the lives of the characters. Or the opening and closing lines show that time is passing through the changing of the seasons.

4.14 Who Is the Main Character?

Directions: Use the list below to plan and write a paragraph in which you explain why you think Anna or Sarah is the main character in this story. Use examples from the book to support your choice.

1. Show how the action revolves around the character you choose.
2. Show how the main character is most affected by what happens.
3. Show how you get to know the character you select better than any other.

   Answers will vary. Sample answers that support each character as the main character are listed on the next page. Student responses should be in paragraph form.

Why Anna is the main character:

Anna is the narrator. Because she is telling the story, it is more her story than anyone else's.

Anna appears in every scene in the story. There are several scenes where Sarah does not appear.

We get to know Anna better than any other character because we know what Anna is thinking. We know only what the other characters say and do.

Anna is most affected by what happens in the story. Anna matures through the events of the story. She is able to admit to herself that she misses her mother. She learns that there will always be something to miss no matter where you are.

Why Sarah is the main character:

The title of the book is an indication that the story is about Sarah more than any other character.

The action revolves around Sarah more than any other character. Papa, Anna, and Caleb all wait to see what Sarah will do.

Sarah is most affected by the action. She is the one who has left her home and moved to an entirely new place. Sarah changes the Witting family, but not as much as moving to the prairie changes Sarah's life.

Sarah talks about herself and her life in Maine more than other characters talk about themselves. Even though we can know what Anna is thinking, we still get to know Sarah better than Anna because she speaks her mind more often.

4.15 Genre: Why Is *Sarah, Plain and Tall* Historical Fiction?

Directions: List some details from the book that show why *Sarah, Plain and Tall* should be classified as historical fiction. A sample has been provided for you on pages 132–133.

Answers will vary. Sample answers are provided.

Characters: Give examples of how the main characters behave in ways that are consistent with the time period. Find out if any of the characters are actual historical figures and list them too. (Ask a parent, teacher, or reading coach to help you determine this.)

Papa, Sarah, Anna, and Caleb all send letters back and forth as a means of communication. Sarah has been living with her brother, but now that he is getting married, she must find somewhere else to live. Living alone is not an option for her. Sarah comes by train to the Wittings' home. Papa uses a wagon to fetch Sarah from the train station. Anna and Caleb wash in a wooden tub. They go to school only during the winter because they must work on the farm during the other seasons. None of the characters are actual historical figures.

Setting: List some of the clues that tell you the historical time period. List some of the clues that tell you where this story occurs.

Anna looks out the window at the prairie. This is a clue that the story is set in the Midwest. The types of flowers the children pick with Sarah also point to the Midwest. The windmill also suggests a farm where the wind can be used for energy. Using the mail to communicate and the wagon and train for travel point to the time period. The wooden tub is a clue that the Wittings do not have indoor plumbing. Jacob plows the field with a team of horses.

Dialogue: Give examples of some of the things the characters say that are expressions people used during this time period. Give examples of some of the things the characters talk about that people during this time period knew a lot about.

Papa talks about taking the horses into town. The song Sarah teaches them is an old folk song. Caleb says that "windmill" was his first word. The children talk about going to school during the winter and driving to school in the wagon or walking three miles. The subjects they mention are writing and sums. This also points to the past.

Plot: List some of the events that happen in the story that are unlikely to happen today. List some of the events in the story that really did occur in this time and place in history.

The main event in the story is that Jacob Witting has advertised for a mail-order bride in the newspaper. Sarah Elisabeth Wheaton has responded to his ad and says she will come for a month to see. This event is very unlikely to happen today, but it is something that did happen when pioneers were first settling on the prairie. If a spouse died, which was common, it was important for the remaining spouse to remarry because of all the work that had to be done on a farm. Damaging storms still occur in the Midwest, but farms are better protected from them than they were during the late 1800s.

Conflict: Describe the main problem the main character faces in the story. Explain how this problem is typical of this time period.

The main problem facing the characters is whether or not Sarah will decide to become a part of the Witting family. It was not uncommon for a mail-order bride to have a trial period once she had met her potential husband before she committed to marrying him. Single women during this time period did have limited choices. Becoming a mail-order bride was one possibility. Like Sarah, most of these women left behind everything they had ever known and traveled to a new place to marry a stranger.

Description: Give examples of some of the historical details in the book, such as possessions, foods, habits, and occupations. List some of the things you learn about life during this time period from reading this book

A dirt road leads to their house. Today most roads are paved—even country roads. The Wittings heat their home with a fireplace. This is still possible today, but not as common as it was a century or more ago. When Anna and Caleb's mother dies, her body is taken away in a wagon. Today a hearse or ambulance would remove someone's body from the home. Anna lights an oil lamp in the evening. The farm has a windmill. Sarah wears a bonnet.

Unit 3:

Note: The answers to the questions in this unit are based on the following edition *of Charlotte's Web:* ISBN 978-0-06-440055-8 (60th Anniversary Edition).

MODULE 6

6.2 The Parts of *Charlotte's Web*

Directions: Examine your copy of *Charlotte's Web* by E. B. White. Answer the questions below based on your examination of the book.

Answers will vary. Sample answers are provided.

1. What do you think is the topic of this book? Where did you find information to help you decide?

   I think the book might be about a spider's web, and a pig, and a girl named Fern. The story takes place on a farm. I found information to help me on the back cover. The title is also a clue.

2. Do you think the title of the book is interesting? What questions do you have about the title?

   I wonder who Charlotte might be. I wonder if a book about a spider's web will be interesting. I wonder if Charlotte's web has special powers.

3. What does the illustration on the cover show? Describe it in your own words.

   The illustration shows a girl holding a pet pig. A goose and a sheep are looking on. The girl and pig are looking at a spider. The pig looks worried.

4. Who created the illustrations? Where did you find this information?

   Garth Williams created the illustrations. I found the information on the front cover.

5. How does the cover illustration give you clues about the book's genre?

   The animals look like they have personalities. This makes me think the animals are characters in the story.

6. What clues on the front and back covers suggest that some things will happen that are not possible in the real world?

   The expressions on the animals' faces on the front cover look like human expressions, not animals'. On the back cover there are words written in the spider's web. The description of the story on the back cover says that the spider is named Charlotte and she puts words about her feelings for the pig in her web. These are all things that cannot happen in the real world.

6.3 Make a Prediction

Directions: Answer the questions below based on the information you collect from the table of contents.

Answers will vary. Sample answers are provided.

1. List some names that might be characters in this story.

   Wilbur, Charlotte, Dr. Dorian, Uncle

2. Write down any chapter titles that give you a clue about the conflict in the story.

   Escape, Loneliness, Bad News

3. During what season of the year do you expect many of the events in the story to occur? Why?

   I think this story takes place during the summer because the chapters suggest events that take place outside. One of the chapters is titled "Summer Days," and another is called "Off to the Fair."

6.4 Read Kate DiCamillo's Foreword

Directions: Read the foreword by Kate DiCamillo. As you read, answer the questions below.

1. Why didn't Kate DiCamillo want to read this book?

   She thought the pig on the front cover looked worried. She assumed that something bad was going to happen in the story.

2. How old was she when she read this book for the first time?

   She was thirty-one.

3. What do you learn about E. B. White from this foreword?

   I learn that E. B. White loved farms, animals, and people. He seemed to love everything about life, even the sad parts.

4. Why does Kate DiCamillo think *Charlotte's Web* is an important book for all of us to read?

   Kate DiCamillo thinks this book shows us how to bear all things by loving all things. She also thinks it teaches us that things will continue, life will go on, and it will be okay.

6.8 Read *Charlotte's Web:* Chapters I–III

Directions: Read chapters I–III of *Charlotte's Web*. These chapters contain the exposition for this story. Remember that *Charlotte's Web* is an animal fantasy, so animals will appear as characters in this story. On the charts below, fill in details E. B. White reveals about the setting and characters.

Answers will vary. Sample answers are provided. It is acceptable for students to also list details from Garth Williams's illustrations as clues to the time and place.

Setting in *Charlotte's Web*	
Details That Tell Me about the Time Period	**Details That Tell Me about the Place**
Mrs. Arable puts a pitcher of cream on the table, instead of a carton. The story takes place quite a few years ago. This is not a modern time period. Fern calls her shoes "sneakers." Mr. Arable dries his hands on a roller towel. Avery is playing with a wooden dagger and air rifle. Even though these toys are still around today, they are considered old-fashioned. A school bus picks up the children for school. Most farms no longer have a woodshed, or if they do, it is rather old. Mr. Arable gives Fern a wooden box to use for Wilbur. Fern has a baby carriage for her dolls instead of a stroller. Mr. Zuckerman pays only $6 for the pig.	Papa goes to the hoghouse. They raise pigs. The following details tell me the story takes place in the country on some farms: The Arables have a woodshed. They have apple trees. They live near a brook where the children can swim. Wilbur goes to live in Mr. Zuckerman's barn. Lots of barn animals are mentioned in chapter 3. Lurvy is a helping hand on the farm. The goose tells Wilbur to run to the nearby woods.

Answers will vary. Sample answers are provided. The following characters appear in the first three chapters: Fern, Mrs. Arable, Papa, Avery, Wilbur, the goose, Mrs. Zuckerman, Mr. Zuckerman, Lurvy, and many of the barnyard animals.

Character Introductions in *Charlotte's Web*

Characters in the Book	What I Think This Character Is Like	Details in the Book That Make Me Think This
Fern	passionate, emotional, loving, imaginative, quiet	She is very upset by the thought of Papa killing the smallest pig. She yells and cries in the first chapter. She takes good care of Wilbur. She treats him as if he is human. She can't eat until he has a drink of milk. She enjoys going to the barn to watch the animals instead of playing with her friends.
Mrs. Arable	practical, kind	She explains why the pig must be killed without any emotion. She makes sure Fern takes responsibility for Wilbur's care. She does give Fern the things she needs to take care of him.
Papa	soft-hearted, practical	He is gentle with Fern when she is so upset about the pig. He changes his mind. He looks at her lovingly. He realizes that Wilbur can't stay at their home. He must go to a farm.
Avery	active, demanding, sarcastic	He comes to breakfast with his air rifle and wooden dagger. He wants a pig too. He says the pig is a "*fine* specimen of a pig," but he means the opposite.
Wilbur	restless, young, naive	He is bored when Fern is away at school. He is "not much more than a baby." He listens to the goose right away and escapes without hesitation.
goose	repetitive, trouble-maker, bossy	She repeats all her words. She convinces Wilbur to escape just to create some excitement. She gives Wilbur orders to help him avoid getting caught.

6.10 Aha! Chapters I–III

Directions: Use the lines provided to answer these questions about chapters I–III. Refer to the chapters as you answer them. To answer some of the questions, you will need to make an inference 🔍. (Draw a conclusion based on the clues in the story and what you already know.)

Chapter I

1. Why is Mr. Arable going to kill the newborn pig? (page 1)

   Mr. Arable is going to kill the pig because he is a runt. He is very small and weak and would probably die anyway.

2. 🔍 What does Fern's reaction to this situation tell you about her character?

   Answers will vary. Sample answers are provided.

   She is a passionate person. She thinks that it is wrong to kill something just because it is a weakling. She is not afraid to stand up for what she thinks.

3. What is Mr. Arable's solution to Fern's plea for the newborn pig's life? (page 3)

   Fern has to take care of the pig and nurse it to health.

4. 🔍 Why does Fern blush after the teacher asks her a question at school? (page 7)

   She is daydreaming about her pig and says that Wilbur is the capital of Pennsylvania.

Chapter II

5. Fern carefully cares for Wilbur as he grows. Explain the details you see in the story that show this. (page 8)

   She strokes him, feeds him, and puts him to bed. She warms his milk for him and even puts a bib on him. She holds the bottle so he can drink it.

6. What is the relationship between Wilbur and Fern like? Give three examples from the story to support your answer. (pages 8–10)

   Answers will vary. Sample answers are provided.

   Fern treats Wilbur like he is her baby. She gives him a bottle of warm milk. She takes him for walks in her doll carriage. She likes to put him to bed. She puts a bib on him when she feeds him.

7. Why does Fern think selling Wilbur to the Zuckermans is a good plan? (page 12)

   Answers will vary. Sample answers are provided.

   She thinks it's a good plan because she will still be able to see Wilbur. She thinks that Wilbur will be safe on her uncle's farm.

Chapter III

8. What does Fern do during the afternoons that she visits the barn? (pages 14–15)

   She places a stool in the sheepfold next to Wilbur's pen and watches Wilbur.

9. How does Wilbur react to everyone chasing him? (page 22)

   He is dazed and frightened. He doesn't like being the center of attention. He tries to do what his friends are saying, but he is overwhelmed and starts crying.

10. Explain how Mr. Zuckerman gets Wilbur back in the pigpen. (pages 22–23)

    He brings a pail of warm slops and gradually coaxes him back into the pigpen.

11. How does Wilbur react to being back in the barnyard after his escape? What does this tell you about Wilbur's personality? (pages 23–24)

    Answers will vary. Sample answers are provided.

    He is peaceful and happy to be home. He is also sleepy. This tells me that he is naturally cautious and shy.

6.11 Reading Strategies: Denotations and Connotations of Words

Directions: On the next two pages, study the following sentences from *Charlotte's Web*. First, think of the images and experiences that you picture when you read the underlined word. Then decide what emotions you associate with the word and write them on the line provided. Finally, circle whether the connotations of the word are positive, negative, or neutral. Discuss your answers with a parent, teacher, or reading coach.

Answers will vary. Sample answers are provided. Further explanation for why the word has positive, negative, or neutral connotations is also provided.

1. "A weakling makes trouble." (page 3)

   Images and experiences I picture when I read this word: someone getting beaten up, someone who is sickly and tired, someone who needs a lot of care

   Emotions I associate with this word: fear, worry, needy

   Connotations (circle one): positive, negative, neutral

   (Someone who is a weakling is not strong. Being a weakling is not an admirable trait.)

2. He was heavily armed—an air rifle in one hand, a wooden dagger in the other. (page 4)

   Images and experiences I picture when I read this word: soldiers, bank robbers, children playing a war game outside

   Emotions I associate with this word: fear, amusement, caution, aggression

   Connotations (circle one): positive, negative, neutral

   (Someone who is "heavily armed" is considered a threat and dangerous. Because Avery is armed only with toy weapons, this description of him is also funny. The negative connotation of "heavily armed" is what creates the humor.)

3. He would stand and gaze up at her with adoring eyes. (page 8)

   Images and experiences I picture when I read this word: looking at something beautiful, someone looking at someone with love, looking at something for a long time

   Emotions I associate with these words: love, warmth, friendliness

   Connotations (circle one): positive, negative, neutral

   ("Gaze" and "adoring" are words often used about someone who is looking at something or someone they love.)

4. . . . her Aunt Edith hollered for Uncle Homer, and Uncle Homer came in from the barn and talked to Fern. (page 12)

   Images and experiences I picture when I read this word: someone who is angry, someone who is being loud

   Emotions I associate with this word: surprise, anger

   Connotations (circle one): positive, negative, neutral

   (It is considered impolite to holler. The verb "holler" has more of a negative connotation than "shout.")

5. Wilbur's new home was in the lower part of the barn, directly underneath the cows. (page 14)

   Images and experiences I picture when I read this word: a hearth, a family having fun in their house, a large family celebrating a holiday together

   Emotions I associate with this word: love, care, laughter, friendliness

   Connotations (circle one): positive, negative, neutral

   ("Home" has positive connotations. It is warmer than the word "house." A home suggests not just a place where we have shelter, but also a place where we are loved.)

6.12 Word Sleuth: Chapters I–III

Directions: Using clues from the surrounding sentences in the book, make an educated guess (inference) about the meaning of the underlined word in each sentence taken from chapters I–III of *Charlotte's Web*. Write it on the line provided. When you have finished, look up the word in the *Readers in Residence* dictionary in the back of this volume. Compare your educated guess with the definition there, and write the dictionary definition on the lines provided.

1. "This is the most terrible case of <u>injustice</u> I ever heard of." (page 3)

   injustice (n.)

   Dictionary definition: **Something that is wrong or unfair.**

2. "That's a *fine* <u>specimen</u> of a pig—it's no bigger than a white rat." (page 5)

   specimen (n.)

   Dictionary definition: **An example of a particular kind of thing.**

3. She just sat and stared out of the window, thinking what a <u>blissful</u> world it was. . . . (page 7)

   blissful (adj.)

   Dictionary definition: **Filled with joy.**

4. It smelled of the <u>perspiration</u> of tired horses. . . . (page 13)

   perspiration (n.)

   Dictionary definition: **Sweat.**

5. The cocker spaniel heard the <u>commotion</u> and he ran out from the barn to join the chase. (page 18)

   commotion (n.)

   Dictionary definition: **Loud disturbance.**

6. Poor Wilbur was dazed and frightened by this <u>hullabaloo</u>. (page 22)

   hullabaloo (n.)

   Dictionary definition: **Uproar.**

7. "He's appealing to your stomach." (page 22)

   appealing (v.)

   Dictionary definition: Entreating, asking for aid.

6.13 Conventions: I Spy Italics

Directions: Find where the words or sentences in the chart below are italicized in the foreword or chapter I and make an inference about the rule the author is following.

I Spy Italics		
Italicized Word(s)	**Page #**	**Why I Think These Words Are in Italics**
Charlotte's Web	foreword	This is the title of a book.
. . . an ax *and* a worried pig!	foreword	The word "and" is italicized so that readers know to emphasize it when they read it.
These autumn days will shorten and grow cold. The leaves will	foreword	These sentences are italicized to show readers that this is a direct quote from the book.
"Do *away* with it?" shrieked Fern. "You mean *kill* it?"	page 1	The words "away" and "kill" are italicized to show readers that Fern emphasized them when she said them.
"That's a *fine* specimen of a pig—it's no bigger than a white rat."	pages 4–5	The word "fine" is italicized to show that Avery emphasized it. He did this to show that he meant the word sarcastically.

6.14 Read *Charlotte's Web*: Chapters IV–VII

Directions: Read chapters IV–VII in *Charlotte's Web*. In this section, E. B. White introduces the last major character in the story. The exposition stage of the plot will conclude, and the inciting incident will occur. Be alert for the event that will trigger the rest of the action. (Look at the chapter titles. You will find a clue among them.)

As you read, notice how the characters display both human and animal behaviors. Use the chart on the next page to list some of the examples of both that you find as you read.

Answers will vary. Sample answers are provided.

Animal and Human Behaviors in *Charlotte's Web*		
Character	**Examples of Animal Behavior**	**Examples of Human Behavior**
Wilbur	His breakfast consists of leftover food scraps that a pig would eat. He lies down in manure. The next morning he eats all the slops Lurvy puts in his trough.	Wilbur plans to talk with Templeton. Wilbur plans to think about what it is like to be alive. He calls for Templeton, who doesn't answer. He cries because he is lonely. He asks the goose what time it is.
Templeton	He spends his time eating, gnawing, hiding, and spying. He disappears into a tunnel he has dug. He sleeps during the daytime and is active at night.	Templeton tells Wilbur he is not interested in playing with him. Templeton goes off on an errand.
the goose	She sits on her eggs and cannot leave until her eggs hatch. She moves around in her nest to get more comfortable.	She tells Wilbur the time. She explains how long it will take for her eggs to hatch. She thinks about how Wilbur doesn't know he is going to be butchered.

Animal and Human Behaviors in *Charlotte's Web*		
Character	**Examples of Animal Behavior**	**Examples of Human Behavior**
Charlotte	She stays in her spider web. She catches a fly and eats it.	Charlotte speaks to Wilbur. She says she will be his friend. She waves to Wilbur from her web. She explains how she catches food in her web.

6.16 Aha! Chapters IV–VII

Directions: Use the lines provided to answer these questions about chapters IV–VII. Refer to the chapters as you answer them. To answer some of the questions, you will need to make an inference 🔍 . (Draw a conclusion based on the clues in the story and what you already know.)

Chapter IV

1. Who is Templeton and where does he live? (page 26)

   Templeton is a rat who lives under Wilbur's trough.

2. Wilbur thinks this is the worst day of his life. (page 31) What are some of the things that happen in this chapter to make him feel this way?

   It rains, he gets wet, and his trough has an inch of water in it. Templeton is nowhere to be seen. Wilbur says one day is just like another. He has no real friends, and he thinks that Fern won't come to visit because of the rain. None of the barnyard animals will play with him. Lurvy forces him to take medicine. Templeton eats his breakfast. Wilbur realizes how lonely he is.

Chapter V

3. Describe some of the sounds Wilbur hears in the barn at night. (page 32)

   He hears Templeton gnawing a hole in the grain bin. He hears the goose turning on her nest and chuckling to herself. He hears the slight scraping of the weather-vane just before dawn.

4. Describe Wilbur's new friend. (pages 37–41) Include at least three different details.

   She uses big words when she speaks. She is a large gray spider. She catches flies and other bugs for food. She spins her web. She is a trapper. According to Wilbur she is "fierce, brutal, scheming, and bloodthirsty."

5. The goose thinks to herself, "There are a lot of things Wilbur doesn't know about life." (page 40) Give two examples from this chapter that show Wilbur doesn't know things the other animals in the barn know.

   He doesn't understand why Templeton is up at night. He doesn't know how long it takes for the goose's eggs to hatch. He doesn't know that his new friend may still be sleeping in the morning. He doesn't know that spiders must kill their prey to survive. He doesn't know he will be killed at Christmastime.

6. Wilbur thinks, "But what a gamble friendship is!" (page 41) A gamble is a risk. Why do you think Wilbur thinks friendship is a risk?

   Answers will vary. Sample answers are provided.

   Wilbur thinks that friendship is a risk because Charlotte has a lot of qualities he doesn't like. Even if he puts time into being friends with Charlotte, he may find he doesn't like her. Then he will have wasted his time.

Chapter VI

7. Why are the early summer days "the happiest and fairest days" on the farm? (page 42)

   Answers will vary. Sample answers are provided.

   The lilacs bloom and the air smells sweet. The bees visit the apple trees. The days grow warm and soft. School ends and the children have time to play. Avery often brings home a trout he has caught to fry.

8. What warning does Charlotte give about the egg that doesn't hatch? (page 47) Why do you think this information may turn out to be important?

   Answers will vary. Sample answers are provided.

   Charlotte says that if the egg ever breaks, the whole barn will smell. Maybe the egg will break at some point in the story.

9. Describe Templeton. Why do you think E. B. White includes so much information about this particular character?

   Answers will vary. Sample answers are provided.

   Templeton is crafty and sneaky. He has no morals. He collects everything and stores it in his lair. It doesn't seem to bother him that the other animals find him disgusting. E. B. White includes a lot of information about Templeton because he is one of the major characters in the story. Perhaps Templeton will do something helpful before the end of the story.

Chapter VII

10. Have you noticed that some animals have names and other do not? What do you think this means?

    Answers will vary. Sample answers are provided.

    The animals that have names are major characters in the story. The animals that do not are minor characters.

11. The sheep explains the importance of Wilbur's weight gain to him. What does he say to Wilbur? (page 49)

    The sheep tells Wilbur that Mr. Zuckerman plans to kill him at Christmastime.

12. How does Wilbur react to this information? (pages 49–51)

    Wilbur is very upset. He cries, screams, and yells for help.

13. Who promises to save Wilbur's life? (page 51)

    Charlotte promises to save Wilbur's life.

6.17 Plot: Inciting Incident

Directions: Now you try. Review the early chapters of *Sarah, Plain and Tall*. Can you find the inciting incident? At what moment does the author introduce the conflict that will drive the action of the story from that point forward? Write your answer below with a brief explanation.

The inciting incident occurs when Papa tells Anna and Caleb he has received a response to an advertisement he has placed in the paper for a wife. The question of whether or not Sarah will want to join the Witting family is what makes the reader want to keep reading. It is the problem that needs to be solved in the rest of the book.

6.18 Word Work: Connotations

Directions: Study the following sentences from *Charlotte's Web*. Writers often use combinations of words to create overall connotations. Think about the emotions you associate with the underlined words. On the lines provided, record your answers and indicate whether the connotations of the words are positive, negative, or neutral. Discuss your answers with a parent, teacher, or reading coach.

Chapter IV is titled "Loneliness." What words do you associate with loneliness? Look at some of the words E. B. White uses in this chapter to help create the feeling of loneliness Wilbur talks about.

The images and experiences that students picture will be unique. Sample answers are provided for that part of each question.

1. The next day was <u>rainy</u> and <u>dark</u>. (page 25)

   Images and experiences I picture when I read these words: Everything is wet. I can't go outside. The world looks dreary.

   Emotions I associate with these words: sad, lonely, bored

   Connotations (circle one): positive, (negative,) neutral

2. When the sheep <u>tired</u> of standing in the rain, they <u>walked slowly</u> up the lane and into the fold. (page 25)

Images and experiences I picture when I read these words: someone dragging his feet, someone whose shoulders are hunched over, the sheep walking with their heads down

Emotions I associate with these words: weary, discouraged, sad

Connotations (circle one): positive, (negative,) neutral

3. Drops of rain struck his face. His yard was cold and wet. (page 27)

   Images and experiences I picture when I read these words: someone flinching, someone just letting the water run down his face, someone shivering

   Emotions I associate with these words: depressed, chilly, sad

   Connotations (circle one): positive, (negative,) neutral

Now look at some of the words E. B. White uses to describe Templeton.

4. "I never do those things if I can avoid them," replied the rat, sourly. (page 29)

   Images and experiences I picture when I read these words: a rat that is hiding in a corner, someone running away, someone hitting the rat

   Emotions I associate with these words: repulsed, distrusting, disgusted

   Connotations (circle one): positive, (negative,) neutral

5. "I prefer to spend my time eating, gnawing, spying, and hiding." (page 29)

   Images and experiences I picture when I read these words: a rat chewing something hard, someone looking around a corner trying not to be seen

   Emotions I associate with these words: revolted, distaste, suspicion

   Connotations (circle one): positive, (negative,) neutral

6. And Templeton, the rat, crept stealthily along the wall and disappeared. (page 30)

   Images and experiences I picture when I read these words: someone being very quiet and sneaky, someone about to be surprised

Emotions I associate with these words: dislike, distrust, caution

Connotations (circle one): positive, negative, neutral

7. How do you think E.B. White wants to make his readers feel about Templeton?

   E. B. White doesn't want readers to trust or admire Templeton. He wants them to be suspicious of Templeton and his intentions. Readers should view Templeton with disgust.

6.19 Word Sleuth: Chapters IV–VII

Directions: Using clues from the surrounding sentences in the book, make an educated guess (inference) about the meaning of the underlined word in each sentence taken from chapters IV–VII of *Charlotte's Web*. Write it on the line provided. When you have finished, look up the word in the *Readers in Residence* dictionary in the back of this volume. Compare your educated guess with the definition there, and write the dictionary definition on the lines provided.

1. "I am a glutton but not a merry-maker." (pages 29–30)

   glutton (n.)

   Dictionary definition: Someone who eats too much.

2. The tunnel was an example of his skill and cunning. (page 30)

   cunning (n.)

   Dictionary definition: Skill, ingenuity.

3. Friendless, dejected, and hungry, he threw himself down in the manure and sobbed. (page 30)

   dejected (adj.)

   Dictionary definition: Hopeless, sad.

4. "I didn't mean to be objectionable." (page 35)

   objectionable (adj.)

   Dictionary definition: Offensive, distasteful.

5. He lay down meekly in the manure, facing the door. (page 35)

   meekly (adv.)

   Dictionary definition: Mildly, gently.

6. He could hardly believe what he was seeing, and although he detested flies, he was sorry for this one. (page 38)

   detested (v.)

   Dictionary definition: Disliked intensely.

7. "Charlotte is fierce, brutal, scheming, bloodthirsty—everything I don't like." (page 41)

   scheming (adj.)

   Dictionary definition: Crafty, forming plans.

8. "I am sure," she said, "that every one of us here will be gratified to learn that after four weeks of unremitting effort and patience on the part of our friend the goose, she now has something to show for it." (page 44)

   unremitting (adj.)

   Dictionary definition: Not stopping.

9. Even Wilbur, who could eat almost anything, was appalled. (page 47)

   appalled (v.)

   Dictionary definition: Shocked, horrified.

10. "But, my friends, if that ancient egg ever breaks, this barn will be untenable." (page 47)

    untenable (adj.)

    Dictionary definition: Unable to be occupied.

11. Her <u>campaign</u> against insects seemed sensible and useful. (page 48)

campaign (n.)

Dictionary definition: An organized course of action.

12. "There's a regular <u>conspiracy</u> around here to kill you at Christmastime." (page 49)

conspiracy (n.)

Dictionary definition: Secret plan.

MODULE 7

7.1 Character Development: Who Wants What?

Directions: Review what you know about the characters based on what you've read in the first seven chapters. For each character listed on the chart on the next page, identify at least one thing the character wants and one thing that gets in the way of that desire.

Answers will vary. Sample answers are provided.

Who Wants What in *Charlotte's Web*?

Character Name	What the Character Wants	What Is in the Way
Fern Arable	She wants to keep Wilbur as a pet. She wants to spend all her time at the barn with Wilbur.	He is a pig, so he can't be a house pet. He has to live at the Zuckermans' barn. Fern has to go to school.
Mr. Arable	He wants to kill Wilbur because he is a runt. Then he wants to sell Wilbur because he has gotten too big and is eating too much.	Fern's love for Wilbur prevents him from doing away with Wilbur.

Who Wants What in *Charlotte's Web*?		
Character Name	**What the Character Wants**	**What Is in the Way**
Templeton	He wants to scavenge for food and to be left alone.	Wilbur wants him to talk and play. The gander threatens to harm him if he comes near the goslings.
Charlotte	She wants to keep Wilbur alive.	Mr. Zuckerman plans to kill Wilbur at Christmastime.
Mr. Zuckerman	He wants to butcher him.	Charlotte is coming up with a plan to save Wilbur's life.

7.3 Read *Charlotte's Web*: Chapters VIII–X

Directions: Read chapters VIII–X of *Charlotte's Web*. As you read these chapters, pay close attention to how you feel. Notice when events cause you to feel stress or concern for the characters because you are unsure of how their problems will be solved.

After you finish reading this section, fill out the chart on the next page for three of the characters that appear in these chapters.

Conflict Complications in *Charlotte's Web*		
Character	**Problem**	**How the Problem Gets Worse**
Fern	She wants to spend time at the barn with Wilbur and the other animals.	Her mother is concerned about her because Fern thinks the animals can talk. She plans to talk with Dr. Dorian.
	She doesn't want Avery to capture Charlotte.	Avery breaks the rotten egg while trying to capture Charlotte. Then the barn smells horrible.
Wilbur	Mr. Zuckerman is planning to kill Wilbur.	Wilbur thinks about being killed more and more, and this makes him frightened.
Charlotte	She has to come up with a plan to save Wilbur's life.	It takes a long time to think of an idea. Avery almost captures her.

7.5 Aha! Chapters VIII–X

Directions: Use the lines provided to answer these questions about chapters VIII–X. Refer to the chapters as you answer them. To answer some of the questions, you will need to make an inference 🔍. (Draw a conclusion based on the clues in the story and what you already know.)

Chapter VIII

1. How does Mrs. Arable react to Fern's stories about the barn animals? What does this show that she thinks about Fern? (pages 52–54)

   Answers will vary. Sample answers are provided.

   She has a worried expression on her face. She thinks Fern is pretending that the animals can talk. She is thinking something must be wrong with Fern. She is concerned that Fern's attachment to Wilbur is not normal.

2. What is Fern's father's reaction? What does this show he thinks about Fern? (page 54)

   Answers will vary. Sample answers are provided.

   He is amused. He thinks Fern has a lively imagination. He isn't concerned about her.

Chapter IX

3. What boast does Wilbur make? (page 56) What character traits best explain why Wilbur makes such a boast?

   Answers will vary. Sample answers are provided.

   Wilbur says he could spin a web if he tried. This shows that Wilbur is immature. Like a young child, he thinks he can do anything. He is a show-off.

4. Why do you think Templeton is willing to help Wilbur with his plan? (page 57)

   Answers will vary. Sample answers are provided.

   I think he is beginning to like Wilbur and he wants to be friends. Or he may find Wilbur's antics amusing.

5. What do Charlotte and Fern think about Wilbur's attempt to prove his boast is true? (pages 57–58)

   They find his attempts to spin a web amusing because they are fond of him. Charlotte is proud of him for continuing to try and not quitting.

6. How does Wilbur's pigpen help Charlotte? (page 57)

   The pigpen attracts flies for Charlotte.

7. How does Wilbur react to the lamb's unkind teasing? (page 61) What does this show about the lamb's character?

   Answers will vary. Sample answers are provided.

   Wilbur's feelings are hurt. He hangs his head and cries. He is embarrassed. The lamb is unkind and thoughtless.

8. Describe how Wilbur's feelings about life on Mr. Zuckerman's farm are changing. Explain why. (pages 62–63)

   Answers will vary. Sample answers are provided.

   He is no longer lonely. He has a friend in Charlotte. He loves his life in the barnyard. He is getting more comfortable there, and he feels like this is home.

9. What do you think Charlotte means when she tells Wilbur, "Never hurry and never worry!"? (page 64) Do you think this is good advice? Why or why not?

   Answers will vary. Sample answers are provided.

   She does not want him to get upset about the thought of being killed. She wants him to trust her to think of a plan and focus on staying healthy. She does not want him to rush her as she thinks about how to save him.

Chapter X

10. What does Charlotte decide to do to save Wilbur's life? (page 67) Why does she think her plan will work?

    She is going to play a trick on Mr. Zuckerman. She thinks it will work because people are gullible.

11. How does Avery create a complication in this chapter? (page 72)

    He tries to capture Charlotte.

12. The title of chapter X is "An Explosion." Explain what this title means now that you've read the chapter. (page 73)

    When Avery tries to capture Charlotte, he trips and the rotten goose egg explodes. This stops Avery from trying to capture Charlotte because the barn smells, and he runs from the barn.

7.6 Word Work: I Spy a Synonym

Look at another example:

> The rat had no morals, no conscience, no scruples, no consideration, no decency, no milk of rodent kindness, no compunctions, no higher feeling, no friendliness, no anything. (page 46)

BOOK EXCERPT

Directions: Answer the questions about the sentence above.

1. What words are unfamiliar to you in this sentence? Write them below.

   Answers will vary.

2. What words do you know?

   Answers will vary.

3. Use the words you do know as clues to help you make an educated guess about the words you do not know.

   Answers will vary.

4. What conclusions can you draw about Templeton's character based on this list of qualities?

   Templeton is self-centered and should not be trusted.

7.7 Word Sleuth: Chapters VIII–X

Directions: Using clues from the surrounding sentences in the book, make an educated guess (inference) about the meaning of the underlined word in each sentence taken from chapters VIII–X of *Charlotte's Web*. Write it on the line provided. When you have finished, look up the word in the *Readers in Residence* dictionary in the back of this volume. Compare your educated guess with the definition there, and write the dictionary definition on the lines provided.

1. "Does he really?" said Mrs. Arable, rather vaguely. (page 53)

   vaguely (adv.)

   Dictionary definition: Unclearly.

2. "Anything to oblige." (page 57)

   oblige (v.)

   Dictionary definition: To do something someone has asked of you.

3. And summoning all his strength, he threw himself into the air, headfirst. (page 58)

   summoning (v.)

   Dictionary definition: Gathering, mustering.

4. "I'm glad I'm a sedentary spider." (page 60)

   sedentary (adj.)

   Dictionary definition: Living in one place, not moving around.

5. "In a forest looking for beechnuts and truffles and delectable roots, pushing leaves aside. . . ." (page 61)

   delectable (adj.)

   Dictionary definition: Tasty, delicious.

6. Wilbur was trembling again, but Charlotte was cool and collected. (page 63)

   collected (adj.)

   Dictionary definition: Composed, in control of one's emotions.

7. "I was just thinking," said the spider, "that people are very <u>gullible</u>." (page 67)

   gullible (adj.)

   Dictionary definition: Easily fooled.

8. "It pays to save things," he said in his <u>surly</u> voice. (page 74)

   surly (adj.)

   Dictionary definition: Grouchy, unfriendly.

9. After a while she <u>bestirred</u> herself. (page 75)

   bestirred (v.)

   Dictionary definition: Roused, stirred up.

7.11 Aha! Chapters XI–XII

Directions: Use the lines provided to answer these questions about chapters XI–XII. Refer to the chapters as you answer them. To answer some of the questions, you will need to make an inference 🔍. (Draw a conclusion based on the clues in the story and what you already know.)

Chapter XI

1. How do Lurvy, Mr. Zuckerman, and Mrs. Zuckerman react when they see Charlotte's web? Use details from the book to support your answer.

   Lurvy feels weak. He stares hard at Charlotte's web. He thinks he is seeing things. He drops to his knees and says a prayer. When Mr. Zuckerman sees the words in the web, he and Lurvy both start to tremble. They say the words "some pig" over and over. They stare at the web, and they stare at Charlotte. When Mrs. Zuckerman comes to look at the web, the three of them stand for almost an hour staring at the words in the web.

2. 🔍 To whom does Mr. Zuckerman talk about the extraordinary events on his farm? Why do you think he chose this person? (page 82)

   Answers will vary. Sample answers are provided.

He talks to the minister. He thinks a miracle has occurred at the farm, and he wants the minister to give him advice about what to do.

3. How does Charlotte's trick change things on the farm and in the town? (pages 83–85)

   People come from miles to see the Zuckermans' famous pig. Mr. Zuckerman is so busy entertaining people who come to the farm that he forgets to do his farm work. He wears his good clothes all the time. Wilbur gets an extra meal. Lurvy shaves and gets a haircut. The church is filled.

4. How does Fern feel about this change of events? (page 85)

   She is glad that the trick is working, but she doesn't like that the barn is full of so many people. She liked it better when she could be alone with her animal friends.

5. How does Charlotte's simple action make Wilbur's situation a lot more complicated?

   Everyone knows about Wilbur now, and they think a miracle has taken place at the farm. The farm is becoming an attraction.

Chapter XII

6. What is the purpose of the meeting in the barn? (page 87)

   Charlotte wants the other animals to help her think of more words for her web.

7. Why does Wilbur object to one of the suggestions? (page 89 and 91)

   He says he is not terrific. He is just an average pig.

8. What are some of the changes in the animals you notice in this chapter?

   They are banding together to help Wilbur. They are becoming friends. Wilbur shows humility when he says he is not terrific.

9. How does the old sheep get Templeton to agree to help? (pages 90–91)

   He reminds Templeton that if Wilbur dies, then Wilbur's food trough will go empty. Templeton won't have anything to eat.

7.12 Word Sleuth: Chapters XI–XII

Directions: Using clues from the surrounding sentences in *Charlotte's Web*, make an educated guess (inference) about the meaning of the underlined word in each sentence taken from chapters XI–XII. Write it on the line provided. When you have finished, look up the word in the *Readers in Residence* dictionary in the back of this volume. Compare your educated guess with the definition there, and write the dictionary definition on the lines provided.

1. Charlotte, sleepy after her night's exertions, smiled as she watched. (page 79)

   exertions (n.)

   Dictionary definition: **Vigorous efforts.**

2. Instead, he walked solemnly back up to the house and spoke to his wife. (page 79)

   solemnly (adv.)

   Dictionary definition: **Seriously, formally.**

3. "She's a rather queer child—full of notions." (pages 82–83)

   notions (n.)

   Dictionary definition: **Ideas or opinions.**

4. Lurvy shaved and got a haircut; and his principal farm duty was to feed the pig while people looked on. (page 84)

   principal (adj.)

   Dictionary definition: **Primary, chief.**

5. "I'll appeal to his baser instincts, of which he has plenty." (pages 89–90)

   baser (adj.)

   Dictionary definition: **Less honorable.**

6. "Wilbur's food is your food; therefore Wilbur's destiny and your destiny are closely linked." (page 90)

   destiny (n.)

   Dictionary definition: **Outcome, purpose in life.**

7. "The meeting is now adjourned." (page 91)

adjourned (v.)

Dictionary definition: Closed or ended.

7.13 Conventions: I Spy Punctuation

Directions: Identify the punctuation marks on the chart on the next page. Find each punctuation mark in chapter XI of *Charlotte's Web*. List a page number where each occurs. What rule do you think E. B. White is following when he uses it?

Answers will vary. Sample answers are provided. Students are not expected to know the rules for punctuation. This exercise is to increase students' awareness of punctuation and to help them make inferences about the rules that guide its usage. This will prepare students for learning the formal rules at a later date.

Punctuation Marks in Chapter XI of *Charlotte's Web*

Punctuation Mark	Name of the Punctuation Mark	Page Number Where It Appears	Rule(s) I Think E. B. White Is Following
.	period	all pages 77–85	Use a period at the end of a statement. Use a period after Mr. and Mrs.
!	exclamation point	77, 79	Use an exclamation point to express strong emotion.
?	question mark	78–82	Use a question mark after a question.
,	comma	all pages 77–85	There are many uses of the comma. In general, commas are used to indicate a brief pause. (Practice reading some of the sentences in this chapter that contain commas. Notice how pausing slightly at the comma helps you to understand the sentence.)

Punctuation Marks in Chapter XI of *Charlotte's Web*			
Punctuation Mark	**Name of the Punctuation Mark**	**Page Number Where It Appears**	**Rule(s) I Think E. B. White Is Following**
:	colon	77	Use a colon after a complete statement that introduces a list, a word, a phrase, or another sentence.
" "	quotation marks	78–83	Use quotation marks to mark off direct (word-for-word) speech. Use quotation marks when referring to a specific word or letter. Example: . . . just beyond the word "pig" . . . (page 81).
'	apostrophe	77, 78	Use an apostrophe to create a possessive noun or pronoun. Use an apostrophe to form a contraction.
;	semicolon	84	Use a semicolon to connect two complete statements.
-	hyphen	all pages 77–85	Use a hyphen to link parts of words or words that belong together.
—	dash	79, 80, 82–85	Use a dash to add information or signal an interruption.
. . .	ellipsis	79	Use an ellipsis to show that something has been omitted.

7.14 Plot Reveals Character

Directions: Fill in the missing information on the following chart. The first one has been completed for you.

Character Traits Revealed through Events in *Charlotte's Web*		
Character	**Character Trait I Would Use to Describe This Character**	**Event in the Story So Far That Shows Me This**
Fern	compassionate	In the opening chapter, Fern is upset when she finds out her father intends to kill Wilbur. She insists on caring for him instead.
Avery	careless	He tries to capture Charlotte and ends up slipping and causing the egg to explode.
Wilbur	boastful, immature, young	Wilbur insists that he can spin a web too.
Charlotte	wise	She gives Wilbur good advice such as "never hurry and never worry."
Templeton	helpful, friendly	Templeton fetches some string and ties it around Wilbur's tail so that Wilbur can try to make a web.

MODULE 8

8.2 Read *Charlotte's Web*: Chapters XIII–XIV

Directions: Read chapters XIII–XIV of *Charlotte's Web* by E. B. White. As you read, think about how E. B. White makes us care more deeply about what happens to Wilbur, Charlotte, Fern, and even Templeton. On the chart on the next page, list some of the reasons you care about these four characters after reading these chapters.

Answers will vary. Sample answers are provided.

Reasons I Care	
Character	**Reasons I Care About This Character**
Wilbur	Wilbur is amusing and playful. He loves hearing stories. He asks Charlotte to sing him to sleep.
Charlotte	She works very hard to save Wilbur. She treats Wilbur like her child.
Fern	She would rather be in the barn than anywhere else. She quietly observes the barn animals. Her mother doesn't understand what is going on with her.
Templeton	Even though he grumbles and complains, he is doing more than the other animals to help save Wilbur's life.

8.4 Aha! Chapters XIII–XIV

Directions: Use the lines provided to answer these questions about chapters XIII–XIV. Refer to the chapters as you answer them. To answer some of the questions, you will need to make an inference 🔍. (Draw a conclusion based on the clues in the story and what you already know.)

Chapter XIII

1. List two types of thread spiders produce. What is each one used for? (page 93)

   Spiders spin dry, tough thread to provide a foundation for their web and sticky thread to snare their prey.

2. What instruction does Mr. Zuckerman give to his wife after seeing the new message in Charlotte's web? (page 96) Why do you think he wants to do this?

Answers will vary. Sample answers are provided.

He tells his wife to call the reporter at the newspaper. He wants the news about Wilbur to be in the newspaper. He is enjoying the excitement that Wilbur is creating.

3. Why is Mr. Zuckerman giving Lurvy so much extra work? (pages 96–97)

He wants Wilbur's pen to look attractive because of all the visitors to the farm. He is also planning to take Wilbur to the County Fair, and he wants Lurvy to start making preparations for that.

4. Why does Templeton like the dump? (page 97)

The dump has good hiding places and usually leftover food scraps.

5. Why does Charlotte decide that *radiant* is a good word to describe Wilbur? (pages 100–101)

When she asks him to run around and jump, his skin shines and he is very active. She is not exactly sure what "radiant action" means, but she thinks that at least "radiant" is a good word to describe Wilbur. He says he feels radiant.

6. How does E. B. White show that Wilbur, Charlotte, and Templeton are becoming friends in this chapter?

They spend time together, and they help each other. Even though Templeton grumbles and complains about his part, he still helps Charlotte with her efforts to save Wilbur.

7. How does Charlotte's lullaby at the end of the chapter show that Charlotte knows Wilbur very well? (page 104)

Answers will vary. Sample answers are provided.

The lullaby is about things Wilbur finds comforting—being loved, not being afraid or lonely, being surrounded by the sounds of nature, and sleeping comfortably in his pigpen.

Chapter XIV

8. Why do you think Mrs. Arable wishes Fern would go out to play with other children instead of spending so much time at the Zuckermans' barn? (pages 106–107)

   Answers will vary. Sample answers are provided.

   She is worried because she thinks Fern is imagining the animals are talking. She thinks it isn't normal.

9. Do you think Fern really hears Charlotte talking? Why or why not?

   Answers will vary. Sample answers are provided.

   Yes. Fern repeats what Charlotte has said with a lot of details from the previous chapter.

10. How does Dr. Dorian respond to Mrs. Arable's concerns? (pages 108–109)

    He is not very concerned. He thinks it is just as miraculous that a spider can spin a web in the first place as it is for a word to appear in one. He suggests the idea that maybe animals really can talk but that humans just talk too much to notice.

11. Why does Dr. Dorian think spider webs are miracles? (page 109-110)

    He thinks they are miracles because no one teaches a spider to spin a web.

12. What does Dr. Dorian tell Mrs. Arable that makes her feel better? (page 111)

    He says not to worry if Fern's appetite is good and she is sleeping well. He thinks she will always love animals, but he thinks that she will get interested in boys in a few years.

8.5 Reading Strategies: More Clues in Context

Directions: Look at this photograph of a spider's web. Can you find the orb, radial, and foundation lines based on the clues in the sentences from *Charlotte's Web*? Which ones do you think a spider spins with dry thread and which ones do you think a spider spins with sticky thread? Answer these questions on the lines provided on the next page. Ask a parent, teacher, or reading coach to help you.

The orb lines are circular. The radial lines cut through the orbs. The foundation lines are attached to the twigs. The foundation and radial lines are dry and tough. The orb lines are sticky.

8.6 Word Sleuth: Chapters XIII–XIV

Directions: Using clues from the surrounding sentences in the book, make an educated guess (inference) about the meaning of the underlined word in each sentence taken from chapters XIII–XIV of *Charlotte's Web*. Write it on the line provided. When you have finished, look up the word in the *Readers in Residence* dictionary in the back of this volume. Compare your educated guess with the definition there, and write the dictionary definition on the lines provided.

1. "We must advertise Wilbur's noble qualities, not his tastiness." (page 98)

   noble (adj.)

   Dictionary definition: Admirable, honorable.

2. So Charlotte told him about another cousin of hers who was an aeronaut. (page 103)

   aeronaut (n.)

   Dictionary definition: A balloon pilot.

3. "Oh, it happened all right," replied Fern. "Charlotte never fibs." (page 106)

   fibs (v.)

   Dictionary definition: Lies.

4. "It is a very sociable place." (page 107)

   sociable (adj.)

   Dictionary definition: Friendly, welcoming.

5. Mrs. Arable fidgeted. (page 110)

   fidgeted (v.)

   Dictionary definition: Moved in a restless or nervous way.

6. "It is quite possible that an animal has spoken civilly to me and that I didn't catch the remark because I wasn't paying attention." (page 110)

   civilly (adv.)

   Dictionary definition: Politely.

7. "Let Fern associate with her friends in the barn if she wants to." (page 111)

   associate (v.)

   Dictionary definition: To spend time with.

8.7 Conventions: I Spy a Simple Sentence

Directions: Write the possible reasons we use different types of punctuation marks in sentences on the lines below.

Answers will vary. Sample answers are provided.

Punctuation marks allow writers to tell readers where they should pause or stop when reading. Punctuation marks help writers to show emotion or emphasis. Punctuation marks allow writers to tell their readers important information, such as when someone is speaking or when words are omitted. Writers need words plus punctuation marks to make what they write easy for readers to understand.

Directions: Turn to page 93 in chapter XIII of *Charlotte's Web*. Find the sentences that contain only a period and no other punctuation. There are five of them. Write them on the chart on the next page.

I Spy a Simple Sentence
1. A spider can produce several kinds of thread.
2. Charlotte decided to use her dry thread for writing the new message.
3. Charlotte climbed to a point at the top of the left side of the web.
4. This formed the upright part of the letter T.
5. Her eight legs were very busy helping.

Directions: On the lines provided, list the subject and main verb of each simple sentence from page 93. The first one has been completed for you.

Simple Sentence Parts	
Subject	**Main Verb**
1. spider	1. can produce
2. Charlotte	2. decided
3. Charlotte	3. climbed
4. this	4. formed
5. legs	5. were helping

8.11 Aha! Chapters XV–XVI

Directions: Use the lines provided to answer these questions about chapters XV–XVI. Refer to the chapters as you answer them. To answer some of the questions, you will need to make an inference 🔍 . (Draw a conclusion based on the clues in the story and what you already know.)

Chapter XV

1. Which method in **8.8 Plot: The Tension Is Rising** does E. B. White use to keep the action rising in the opening of chapter XV? Explain your choice. (page 113)

   He uses foreshadowing. He uses the crickets' sad song to suggest that something sad may happen. Like summer, something may come to an end.

2. Make a list of four different characters and their reactions to the crickets' sad song. (pages 113–114)

   Answers will vary. Sample answers are provided. Students have to list only four characters.

The Characters React to the Crickets' Song	
Character	**Reaction to Crickets' Sad Song**
Avery	He knows that soon summer will be over and school will start again.
Fern	She knows that soon summer will be over and school will start again.
the young geese	They know they will never be little goslings again.
Charlotte	She knows she doesn't have much time left to save Wilbur's life.
Mrs. Zuckerman	She sighs because another summer is gone.

The Characters React to the Crickets' Song	
Character	**Reaction to Crickets' Sad Song**
Lurvy	He knows it is time to dig potatoes.
the sheep	They break a hole in the pasture fence and wander into the field across the road.
the gander	He leads his family into the orchard to eat the apples on the ground.

3. What does Wilbur do to make himself look radiant? (pages 114–115)

   He stands in the sunlight. He turns his head slightly and blinks his long eyelashes. He breathes deeply. He does a back flip and half twist.

4. What does Wilbur realize is one of the most satisfying things in the world? (page 115)

   He realizes that friendship is one of the most satisfying things in the world.

5. Why does Wilbur want to distinguish himself at the fair? (page 115)

   He thinks that if he wins some prize money, Mr. Zuckerman will let him live.

6. How does E. B. White make the plot more complicated and increase the tension in chapter XV?

   Charlotte may not go to the fair with Wilbur because it is time for her to lay her eggs.

Chapter XVI

7. How do the characters' dreams the night before the fair show what each one wants? (pages 118–119)

   Answers will vary. Sample answers are provided.

   Avery would like the excitement of being stuck at the top of the Ferris wheel. Fern wants to swing on the swing so many times that she feels sick. Lurvy is looking forward to throwing baseballs to win a blanket. Mrs. Zuckerman is hoping to buy a deep freeze unit. Mr. Zuckerman is hoping that Wilbur will win all the prizes at the fair and be the main attraction.

8. Why does Fern put on her prettiest dress before going to the fair? (page 119) How does this show that Fern is changing?

   Answers will vary. Sample answers are provided.

   She knows that she will see boys at the fair. This is a sign that Fern is getting older.

9. Why does Mrs. Zuckerman decide to give Wilbur a buttermilk bath? How might this action be linked to her dream? (pages 120–121)

   Answers will vary. Sample answers are provided.

   She thinks this will make Wilbur look extra special. Perhaps she hopes to use the prize money to buy a deep freeze.

10. Why does Charlotte decide to go to the fair with Wilbur? Why does she want Templeton to come too? (page 122)

    She thinks something unexpected may happen and someone who knows how to write has to go along. She may need Templeton to run an errand or do other work.

11. Describe how the animals help execute Charlotte's plan. What does their cooperation show has changed in the barnyard? (pages 122–125)

    Answers will vary. Sample answers are provided.

    The old sheep talks Templeton into going to the fair. Even though Templeton still grumbles and complains, you can tell he is being

friendlier than before. He calls Wilbur "Mr. Radiant." The geese serve as lookouts. The sheep tells Wilbur to struggle so Mr. Zuckerman won't think he is bewitched. The geese make a racket to distract attention. This shows that the animals have become friends and are banding together to help save Wilbur's life.

12. How does E. B. White use Mr. Arable to create tension in this chapter? (page 126)

    Mr. Arable says that Mr. Zuckerman will get extra good ham and bacon from Wilbur when it comes time to kill him.

8.12 Word Sleuth: Chapters XV–XVI

Directions: Using clues from the surrounding sentences in the book, make an educated guess (inference) about the meaning of the underlined word in each sentence taken from chapters XV–XVI of *Charlotte's Web*. Write it on the line provided. When you have finished, look up the word in the *Readers in Residence* dictionary in the back of this volume. Compare your educated guess with the definition there, and write the dictionary definition on the lines provided.

1. They sang the song of summer's ending, a sad, <u>monotonous</u> song. (page 113)

   monotonous (adj.)

   Dictionary definition: Repetitive.

2. Wilbur was <u>modest</u>; fame did not spoil him. (page 115)

   modest (adj.)

   Dictionary definition: Humble.

3. If he could <u>distinguish</u> himself at the Fair, and maybe win some prize money, he was sure Zuckerman would let him live. (page 115)

   distinguish (v.)

   Dictionary definition: To stand out from others.

4. "I'm versatile." (page 116)

   versatile (adj.)

   Dictionary definition: Able to do many different things.

5. Charlotte gave her web a twitch and moodily watched it sway. (page 116)

   moodily (adv.)

   Dictionary definition: Unhappily.

6. "I knew you wouldn't forsake me just when I need you most." (page 117)

   forsake (v.)

   Dictionary definition: To abandon.

7. "In the trampled grass of the infield you will find old discarded lunch boxes containing the foul remains of peanut butter sandwiches. . . ." (page 123)

   foul (adj.)

   Dictionary definition: Smelly or rotten.

8. "In the hard-packed dirt of the midway, after the glaring lights are out and the people have gone home to bed, you will find a veritable treasure of popcorn fragments. . . ." (page 123)

   veritable (adj.)

   Dictionary definition: Genuine or true.

9. "Is this appetizing yarn of yours true?" (page 123)

   yarn (n.)

   Dictionary definition: A tall tale or story.

10. ". . . I don't want to be stepped on, or kicked in the face, or pummeled, or crushed in any way, or squashed, or buffeted about, or bruised, or lacerated, or scarred, or biffed." (page 125)

    pummeled (v.)

    Dictionary definition: Punched or beaten.

buffeted (v.)

Dictionary definition: Knocked about, pounded.

lacerated (v.)

Dictionary definition: Cut or slashed.

biffed (v.)

Dictionary definition: Hit or punched.

MODULE 9

9.1 Look How Far You've Come

Directions: So far you have ascended through three stages of plot in *Charlotte's Web*. On the chart on the next page, write one or two sentences about what has happened in each stage of the plot so far.

Answers will vary. Sample answers are provided. Students should understand how these events advance the plot.

The Story So Far	
Stage	**What Happened**
Exposition	Fern's father intends to kill a pig that is the runt of the litter with an ax, but Fern stops him. He says Fern must take care of the pig. Fern names the pig Wilbur. When Wilbur grows too large, he goes to live on Mr. Zuckerman's farm.
Inciting Incident	The old sheep tells Wilbur that Mr. Zuckerman is planning to kill him at Christmastime.
Rising Action	Charlotte says she will save Wilbur's life. Fern's mother grows worried about Fern. Avery almost captures Charlotte and breaks the rotten egg in the barn. Charlotte writes the words "Some Pig" in her web, and Wilbur becomes a big attraction. Mr. Zuckerman decides to show Wilbur at the County Fair. Charlotte and Templeton stow away in Wilbur's crate so that they can help him distinguish himself at the fair. Mr. Arable mentions that Mr. Zuckerman will get some fine ham and bacon from Wilbur when he is butchered.

9.2 Plot: Recognizing the Climax

Directions: Reread chapter 9 of *Sarah, Plain and Tall* from the beginning with a parent, teacher, or reading coach. Stop at the word *Slowly* in the middle of page 64. Study carefully how Patricia MacLachlan builds both the emotional tension and the suspense in this scene. Discuss these questions after you read this section.

1. When the chapter opens, what has just happened?

   The storm is over. Anna describes the damage.

2. What promise to Sarah does Papa keep?

   He teaches her how to drive the wagon.

3. How are Caleb and Anna feeling? How can you tell?

   Answers will vary. Sample answers are provided.

   They are worried. Caleb thinks of ways he can prevent her from going. Anna speaks to him crossly. Caleb starts to cry openly. Anna goes in the barn and shouts in anger. Caleb hangs back and watches Sarah and Papa from afar.

4. How is Jacob feeling? How can you tell?

   Answers will vary. Sample answers are provided.

   He is unconcerned that Sarah will leave. He is unaware that Sarah and Caleb are upset. He goes about the business of teaching Sarah to drive the wagon. He asks Caleb to chop some wood and doesn't see his tears. He stands near Sarah while she is sitting in the wagon. He speaks easily to Sarah when she is leaving and says "very good" after she is gone.

5. How can you tell that Caleb's mood changes when he sees the wagon return?

   Answers will vary. Sample answers are provided.

   He shouts, and he climbs from the porch onto the roof. He shouts so everyone can hear that he sees Sarah coming home.

Directions: Discuss with a parent, teacher, or reading coach how Patricia MacLachlan uses one of these options to create a climax.

Patricia MacLachlan creates the climax by having Sarah take action. She insists on learning how to drive the wagon so that she can go to town alone. Caleb and Anna think Sarah will use this opportunity to leave them. After all, it was the wagon that took their mother away. When Sarah returns in the wagon, they know she is coming home. She assures them of this once she realizes how worried they had been.

Sarah learns a lesson when Maggie tells her there is always something to miss no matter where you are, but this doesn't set up the resolution of the central problem—whether or not Sarah will choose to become Anna and Caleb's new mother. So this is not how Patricia MacLachlan creates the climax.

Sarah makes a decision to stay, but we don't know when she makes this decision. She may have decided long before she went to town that she wanted to be Anna and Caleb's mother and Jacob's wife. If an author has a character make a decision to set up the climax of the story, the author will show the character making the decision.

9.3 Plot: Falling Action and Resolution

Directions: Read chapter 9 from the sentence beginning with *Slowly* on page 64 until the end of the book with a parent, teacher, or reading coach. Notice how Patricia MacLachlan shows that the complications have unraveled and the Witting family has returned to a life with no conflict to resolve—at least for the moment. Discuss the following questions after you read this section.

1. How does the mood change with Sarah's return? What clues make you think this?

   Answers will vary. Sample answers are provided.

   The dogs are jumping happily. Nick leaps up to greet her. Caleb bursts into tears and cries, "Seal was very worried!" This is touching and funny.

2. What are some of the remaining questions Patricia MacLachlan answers for the reader after Sarah returns?

   Sarah admits that she will miss her old home, but she isn't going to leave because she would miss them more.

3. How is the gift Sarah has brought for everyone important? What does it mean?

   Answers will vary. Sample answers are provided.

   Sarah has found a way to bring her old life with her to the prairie. We can assume that Jacob, Anna, and Caleb will all experience a part of that life by the sea that Sarah has brought with her. Sarah has found a way to remember her life by the sea so that she will miss it less.

4. How does Patricia MacLachlan indicate the beginning of the resolution to readers?

   It is in italics.

5. What inferences can you make about how each character has changed from studying the resolution of the story?

   Answers will vary. Sample answers are provided.

   There are four at the table by candlelight. They have become a family, and Sarah has made their meals together special. Caleb is nearly asleep because it is late, but he is also relieved that his worries are over. Sarah smiles at Jacob. She has come to love him. Jacob says he will say "ayuh" when the preacher asks if he will have Sarah as his wife. His sense of humor has returned. Anna has matured. She understands that the difficulties of life on the prairie will continue but Sarah will add color to their lives. They will toss curls in the wind for the birds and dry flowers to liven the winter. They will sing, and they will look at Sarah's pictures of the sea on the wall. Anna understands that Sarah will be as committed to them as they are to her.

9.4 Make a Prediction

Directions: Turn to the table of contents for *Charlotte's Web*. Study the titles of the last six chapters in the book. On the chart on the next page, predict which chapters will be a part of the rising action, climax, falling action, and resolution. Briefly state what clues in the chapter titles help you to make this prediction.

Answers will vary. Sample answers are provided.

My Plot Predictions

Chapter Title	My Prediction for Plot Stage	Why
XVIII. The Cool of the Evening	Rising Action	It sounds like the night before the big event at the fair. I imagine Wilbur is worried.
XIX. The Egg Sac	Rising Action	I think Charlotte must lay her eggs in this chapter. Because this is so important, it may affect her ability to help Wilbur.
XX. The Hour of Triumph	Climax	It sounds like the most important event in the story happens in this chapter.
XXI. Last Day	Falling Action	This sounds like something is coming to an end.
XXII. A Warm Wind	Resolution	It sounds like the title of a chapter that shows how things have changed. Wind brings changing weather, so E. B. White might use that title to show change in his story.

9.7 Aha! Chapters XVII–XIX

Directions: Use the lines provided to answer these questions about chapters XVII–XIX. Refer to the chapters as you answer them. To answer some of the questions, you will need to make an inference 🔍. (Draw a conclusion based on the clues in the story and what you already know.)

Chapter XVII

1. Why does Mrs. Arable sigh and blow her nose? (page 133)

   Answers will vary. Sample answers are provided.

   Mrs. Arable is emotional about her children being old enough to go off on their own at the fair.

2. What complication does E. B. White introduce in this chapter?

   Uncle is an enormous pig that Wilbur will have to compete against.

3. What is Charlotte's opinion of the pig named Uncle? (page 135) Why?

   She doesn't like him. She thinks he has a "most unattractive personality." He tells poor jokes, is noisy, is not very clean, and is unpleasant.

4. Why does Charlotte think Uncle will be a hard pig to beat? (page 135)

   Charlotte thinks he will be hard to beat because he is so much bigger than Wilbur.

5. There are many clues that Charlotte isn't feeling well. Write down two that you see. (page 136)

   Answers will vary. Sample answers are provided.

   Charlotte is tired. She doesn't have energy. She is swollen and listless. She takes a nap.

Chapter XVIII

6. What does Charlotte tell Templeton when he leaves the crate for his evening activities? (page 138)

   She tells him to bring her back a word and tonight she will write for the last time.

7. How does E. B. White use foreshadowing in chapter XVIII? (page 140)

   Charlotte says the word Templeton brings back will be the last word she will ever write. It is beginning to feel as though something bad may happen to Charlotte.

8. What word does Templeton bring back for Charlotte? (page 140) Why does Charlotte think this is a good choice?

   He brings back the word "humble." She says this word has two meanings and they both fit Wilbur. He is "not proud" and he is also "near the ground." She is referring to how short he is.

9. How does Charlotte comfort Wilbur that evening? (page 142)

   She assures him that tomorrow he will win a prize and become even more famous. This will make Mr. Zuckerman proud and happy. He won't want to kill the pig that has brought him such good fortune.

10. How does Fern describe the day at the fair to her mother at bedtime? (page 143) Do you think Mrs. Arable is reassured about Fern? Why or why not?

    Answers will vary. Sample answers are provided.

    She says she has had the best time of her whole life. Mrs. Arable is very pleased with this news. The exclamation points show she is happy. She probably thinks Fern is acting like a normal little girl now because she enjoyed spending the day with friends her age.

Chapter XIX

11. How do Charlotte's appearance and condition change overnight? (page 144)

    She is much smaller; she is very quiet and weak.

12. What does Charlotte mean when she refers to the egg sac as her *magnum opus*? Describe what Wilbur sees. (pages 144–145)

    Answers will vary. Sample answers are provided.

    Magnum opus is Latin for one's greatest work. The egg sac looks like a cocoon, and it is peach-colored. It looks like it is made from cotton candy. It is made of the toughest material a spider can produce. It is waterproof, and it contains Charlotte's 514 eggs.

13. Why does Charlotte feel sad after laying her eggs? (page 146)

    She is sad because she won't ever see her children.

14. What does Charlotte mean when she says she is languishing? (page 146) Does Wilbur seem concerned about Charlotte? Write one sentence from the book that shows this.

    She is losing strength. She is getting old. Wilbur is concerned. One sentence that shows this is "But he was so worried he felt he had to ask." He asks her to explain why she won't see her children and also what she means by the word "languishing."

15. Describe how Templeton looks after his first night at the fair? (page 147)

    He is "swollen to twice his normal size." His stomach is as big "as a jelly jar."

16. What bad news does Templeton give to Wilbur? (page 148)

    He says Uncle has already won the blue ribbon for first prize.

17. What is Charlotte's reaction to the announcement made over the loudspeaker? (pages 151–153)

    She is certain that she has saved Wilbur's life. She feels peaceful and contented.

9.8 Word Sleuth: Chapters XVII–XIX

Directions: Using clues from the surrounding sentences in the book, make an educated guess (inference) about the meaning of the underlined word in each sentence taken from chapters XVII–XIX of *Charlotte's Web*. Write it on the line provided. When you have finished, look up the word in the *Readers in Residence* dictionary in the back of this volume. Compare your educated guess with the definition there, and write the dictionary definition on the line provided.

1. "He is too <u>familiar</u>, too noisy, and he cracks weak jokes." (page 135)

   familiar (adj.)

   Dictionary definition: Too friendly, not polite.

2. She looked rather swollen and she seemed listless. (page 136)

   listless (adj.)

   Dictionary definition: Without energy.

3. Templeton's keen nose detected many fine smells in the air. (page 138)

   keen (adj.)

   Dictionary definition: Highly developed, very sensitive.

4. "What is that nifty little thing?" (page 144)

   nifty (adj.)

   Dictionary definition: Useful or attractive.

5. "What makes you sound so down-hearted?" (page 146)

   down-hearted (adj.)

   Dictionary definition: Discouraged.

6. "I think I'm languishing, to tell you the truth." (page 146)

   languishing (v.)

   Dictionary definition: Having one's health decline or fail.

7. "What feasting and carousing!" (page 148)

   carousing (v.)

   Dictionary definition: Wander about celebrating and enjoying oneself.

8. "A real gorge!" (page 148)

   gorge (n.)

   Dictionary definition: A big feast where people overeat.

9. "It would serve you right if you had an acute attack of indigestion." (page 148)

   acute (adj.)

   Dictionary definition: Painful and severe.

9.9 Read *Charlotte's Web*: Chapters XX–XXII

Directions: Read chapters XX–XXII of *Charlotte's Web*. This section of the story contains the conclusion of the climax, the falling action, and the resolution. Use the chart below to list the events that occur during each of these stages of the plot.

Events in Each Plot Stage	
Stage	**Events**
climax	Wilbur receives a special prize in front of everyone in the grandstands. Mr. Zuckerman thinks this is the greatest moment of his life. Charlotte knows that her work is done and Wilbur will not be killed.
falling action	Charlotte assures Wilbur that he is now safe. Charlotte explains the importance of friendship to Wilbur. She then explains that she will shortly die. Wilbur is distraught. He solicits Templeton's help in bringing her egg sac back to the farm. Charlotte dies alone the next day.
resolution	Wilbur misses Charlotte, but his life is happy. The animals are all friendlier with each other, even Templeton. In the spring, Charlotte's children are born. Wilbur watches over them until one windy day when almost all of them sail away, except for three who choose to stay in the barnyard with Wilbur. Some of Charlotte's descendants continue to live in the barn with Wilbur the rest of his days. Wilbur is never killed and is happy.

9.11 Chapters XX–XXII

Directions: Use the lines provided to answer these questions about chapters XX–XXII. Refer to the chapters as you answer them. To answer some of the questions, you will need to make an inference 🔍. (Draw a conclusion based on the clues in the story and what you already know.)

Chapter XX

🔍 1. Where is Fern while Wilbur is getting his award? (page 156) Do you find this surprising? Why or why not?

Answers will vary. Sample answers are provided.

She is looking for Henry Fussy so they can ride the Ferris wheel again. This is surprising because she is missing Wilbur's biggest moment.

2. Charlotte overhears all that is going on, and the words give her courage. (pages 156–157) Why do you think she needs courage?

   Answers will vary. Sample answers are provided.

   Charlotte knows she is going to die. Knowing that she has saved Wilbur's life gives her the courage to face her death and the loss of her friendship with Wilbur.

3. Whose hour of triumph is this? Why? (pages 156–157)

   Answers will vary. Sample answers are provided.

   This is Charlotte's hour of triumph. Wilbur is considered a special pig only because of the words Charlotte has woven about him in her web. She has fulfilled her promise to save his life.

4. What prize does Mr. Zuckerman receive from the judges at the grandstand? What does Wilbur receive from them? (pages 158 and 160)

   Mr. Zuckerman receives $25 from the judges. Wilbur receives a bronze medal.

5. Wilbur appears to be nervous about receiving his award at the grandstand. Give details from the book that show this. (pages 158–160)

   First Wilbur blushes. Then he feels dizzier and dizzier. When the crowd bursts into applause and cheers, he faints.

6. Why is this experience the greatest moment in Mr. Zuckerman's life? (page 160)

   Answers will vary. Sample answers are provided.

   He finds it thrilling to win a prize in front of a large audience.

Chapter XXI

7. Why does Charlotte believe that Mr. Zuckerman will not harm Wilbur now? (pages 163–164)

Answers will vary. Sample answers are provided.

She says that Wilbur "means a great deal" to Mr. Zuckerman now. Wilbur is responsible for Mr. Zuckerman's finest hour, and Wilbur is now famous. There would probably be an uproar if Mr. Zuckerman killed Wilbur.

8. How has Wilbur's attitude toward Charlotte changed throughout the story, from the beginning to the end? Provide details from the book. (pages 41, 164, and 173)

At first Wilbur believes that "Charlotte is fierce, brutal, scheming, bloodthirsty." However, later Wilbur tells Charlotte that he "would gladly give my life for you." His final opinion of Charlotte is that "no one had ever had such a friend" as Charlotte.

9. Explain in your own words why Charlotte devoted herself to saving Wilbur's life. (page 164)

Answers will vary. Sample answers are provided.

Charlotte likes Wilbur and wants to help her friend. She feels like a mother toward Wilbur. She also realizes that she has talents and skills she can use to save Wilbur's life. She wants to use her gifts for someone else's good.

10. Why isn't Charlotte returning to the farm with Wilbur? (page 165)

She knows she will die soon. She doesn't have the energy to move.

11. What idea does Wilbur have about Charlotte's children? (page 166)

Wilbur decides to bring her egg sac back to the farm and take care of it.

12. How does Wilbur motivate Templeton to help get Charlotte's egg sac down from the ceiling? (page 168)

    He promises that if Templeton will help him, he will always let Templeton eat first from the trough.

13. What is the cause of Charlotte's death?

    Answers will vary. Sample answers are provided.

    The text doesn't say exactly. She dies either of old age or of exhaustion from the effort required to create her egg sac. (Barn spiders like Charlotte typically die after laying their eggs.)

Chapter XXII

14. On page 176 you read that nothing is as important to Wilbur as the egg sac. Why do you think the egg sac is so important to him?

    Answers will vary. Sample answers are provided.

    The egg sac represents Charlotte and their friendship. It's one way he can keep Charlotte's memory alive. Taking care of Charlotte's "magnum opus" is one way he can show his love for Charlotte and his appreciation for what she did to save his life. He already loves her babies because he loved her so much.

15. What sound signals the beginning of spring? (page 176)

    The sound of the frogs croaking is the signal for spring.

16. What does "We take to the breeze, we go as we please" describe? (page 180)

    This describes how the young spiders make balloons that can catch the breeze and carry them away.

17. What are the names of the three spiders that stay at the barn with Wilbur? Where do their names come from? (pages 181–182)

    Joy chooses this name for herself because Wilbur says he is trembling with joy. Aranea chooses this name because her mother's middle initial was A. The last spider asks Wilbur to give her a name, and he chooses Nellie.

18. Do Charlotte's descendants ever take her place in Wilbur's heart? Why or why not? (page 184)

Answers will vary. Sample answers are provided.

Wilbur loves Charlotte's children and grandchildren, but they never take her place in his heart. She was unique and special. She was too good a friend to Wilbur to ever be replaced.

19. Do you think the author, E. B. White, liked farm life? Explain your answer.

Answers will vary. Sample answers are provided.

Yes, it is very clear that E. B. White loved animals and life on a farm. He explains many parts of farm life with love and specific details. It is obvious from how he describes the seasons, animals, smells, and sounds in *Charlotte's Web* that E. B. White loved God's world.

9.12 Word Sleuth: Chapters XX–XXII

Directions: Using clues from the surrounding sentences in the book, make an educated guess (inference) about the meaning of the underlined word in each sentence taken from chapters XX–XXII of *Charlotte's Web*. Write it on the line provided. When you have finished, look up the word in the *Readers in Residence* dictionary in the back of this volume. Compare your educated guess with the definition there, and write the dictionary definition on the lines provided.

1. "Special announcement!" said the loud speaker in a <u>pompous</u> voice. (page 155)

   pompous (adj.)

   Dictionary definition: Self-important.

2. " . . . calling the attention of all and <u>sundry</u> to the fact that this pig was completely out of the ordinary." (page. 157)

   sundry (n.)

   Dictionary definition: Different, various.

3. "This miracle has never been fully explained, although learned men have visited the Zuckerman pigpen to study and observe the phenomenon." (page 157)

   phenomenon (n.)

   Dictionary definition: Wonder or marvel.

4. "For goodness' sake!" bellowed Mr. Zuckerman. . . (page 161)

   bellowed (v.)

   Dictionary definition: Shouted.

5. "By helping you, perhaps I was trying to lift up my life a trifle." (page 164)

   trifle (n.)

   Dictionary definition: A small amount.

6. "And I thank you for your generous sentiments." (page 165)

   sentiments (n.)

   Dictionary definition: Feelings, judgments.

7. Great sobs racked his body. (page 165)

   racked (v.)

   Dictionary definition: Afflicted.

8. The sheds and buildings were empty and forlorn. (page 171)

   forlorn (adj.)

   Dictionary definition: Sad and lonely.

9. "You have chosen a hallowed doorway from which to string your webs." (page 182)

   hallowed (adj.)

   Dictionary definition: Holy, blessed, highly respected.

10. It was the best place to be, thought Wilbur, this warm delicious cellar, with the garrulous geese. . . . (page 183)

garrulous (adj.)

Dictionary definition: Long-winded, talkative.

9.13 Recognizing the Climax of *Charlotte's Web*

Directions: Sketch or describe one event from each of the plot stages in *Charlotte's Web* using the plot diagrams provided on the next two pages.

Answers will vary. Sample answers are provided.

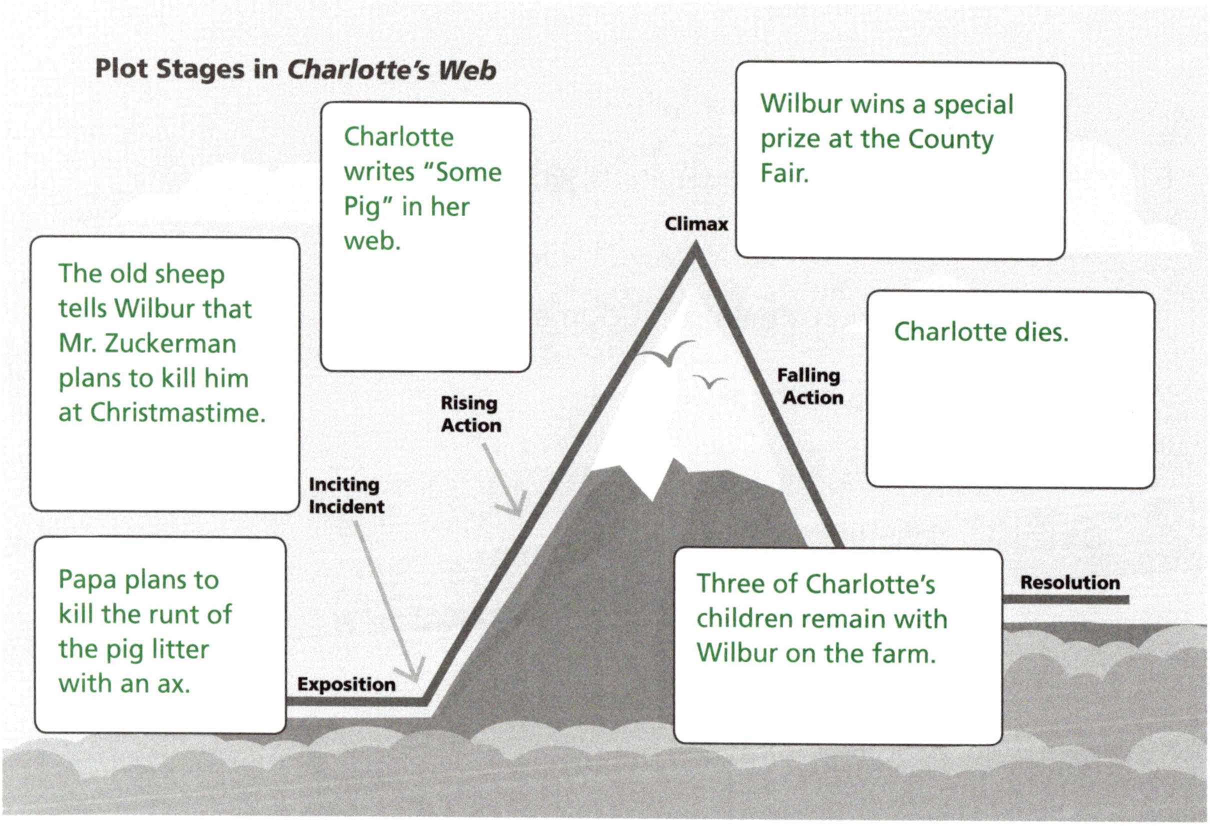

9.14 Genre: Why Is *Charlotte's Web* an Animal Fantasy?

Directions: Go back to **6.1** Introduction to Animal Fantasy and look over the infographic about animal fantasy. In the space below, list some details from the book that show you *Charlotte's Web* should be classified as an animal fantasy.

Answers will vary. Sample answers are provided.

Characters: Give examples of how the animal characters have human characteristics. Give examples of how the animal characters have animal characteristics. Name any human characters who are able to talk with or understand the animals.

Most of the animals in the story can talk. Wilbur and Charlotte, in particular, talk about things humans discuss. They talk about friendship, love, risk, and adventure. Charlotte is as intelligent as a human being. She knows a lot of big words, and she can read. Templeton can read some of the words on the papers he finds too. The animal characters live in the barn and eat the food that animals eat. They sleep where animals sleep. Apart from Charlotte spinning words in her web, the animals can't do anything physically that only humans can do. Fern is the only human who can hear the animals talk, though she never talks with the animals directly.

Setting: Describe the place where the story occurs. If the story takes place in the real world or the animal's habitat, explain the clues that show you this.

The setting is realistic. Most of the story takes place in the barn. The barn has a manure pile, a hayloft, a trough for food, and stalls for the animals. E. B. White also gives details about the changing seasons, such as the lilacs blooming in early summer and the crickets' song at summer's end.

Dialogue: Give examples of the conversations among the animals that are similar to human conversation. List some of the topics, emotions, humor, and relationships revealed through their conversations.

Charlotte and Wilbur talk to each other like humans. When they first meet, Charlotte introduces herself to Wilbur. Then she describes what she does for a living. Wilbur boasts he can make a spider web too, and Charlotte and

Templeton enjoy watching him attempt this. Charlotte sings Wilbur lullabies and tells him stories, just as humans do with young children.

Plot: Show how the events in the story are similar to events in human lives.

Most of the plot is about saving Wilbur's life from the farmer's ax, which is not an event typical to human lives. The following events are similar to events in human lives: Wilbur is lonely. Wilbur makes friends with Charlotte. Charlotte helps Wilbur solve his problem with a complex plan. The other animals gradually become friends. Templeton becomes a better rat and gets along with the others. Wilbur takes care of Charlotte's children.

Conflict: Describe the main conflict facing the major animal characters. Describe how human actions affect the animals' lives.

The main conflict is that Mr. Zuckerman intends to butcher Wilbur for his meat. This is what happens to most pigs. The humans also take Wilbur to the fair, where they put him on display. Avery almost captures Charlotte, and he breaks Templeton's egg.

Description: List some of the details in the story that are appropriate to the time and place of the story. Describe any details about the animals that are actually human characteristics.

There are details about the time and place on almost every page. This is one reason the story is so famous. Here are a few examples: The barn is described as old. It smells of hay and manure. "It smelled of grain and of harness dressing and of axle grease and of rubber boots and of new rope." The Country Fair is described as smelling of dust from the racecars. There are "hamburgers frying" and "balloons aloft." The animals do not have any clothes or possessions that are out of character for the types of animals they are.

Unit 5:

Note: The answers to the questions in this unit are based on the following edition of *Because of Winn-Dixie:* ISBN 978-0-7636-8086-2.

MODULE 11

11.1 The Cover of *Because of Winn-Dixie*

Directions: Examine your copy of *Because of Winn-Dixie* by Kate DiCamillo. Answer the questions below based on your preview of the book.

1. Do you think the title of the book is interesting? Do you have questions about the title? If so, what are they?

   Answers will vary. Sample answers are provided.

   I wonder who Winn-Dixie is and what happened because of him.

2. Does the cover illustration seem to be a real or imaginary event?

   Answers will vary. Sample answers are provided.

   The image on the cover is realistic. The haziness of the background adds a dreamlike quality.

3. Is there any additional information on the cover? List some of it.

   An image of the Newbery Honor award appears on the front cover. The back cover includes a synopsis of the story and a quote from a review.

4. Who are some of the characters you expect to meet in this book?

   I expect to meet a girl named Opal, a dog, and Opal's friends.

5. What events do you think the plot may include?

   Answers will vary. Sample answers are provided.

   I think the story will include when Opal meets Winn-Dixie. It will include when Opal meets some of her unusual new friends.

6. Read the author's biography on the inside of the back cover. What awards has she received for her writing? List them.

   Kate DiCamillo has won the Newbery Medal. One of her books was also a National Book Award Finalist.

11.6 Setting: *Charlotte's Web*

Directions: Now think about the setting of *Charlotte's Web*. Refer back to the book to answer the following questions.

1. What is the time period for *Charlotte's Web*? List three clues that help you decide.

   Answers will vary. Sample answers are provided. The clues in the sample answers should allow students to identify the time period as before they were born but more recent than when *Sarah, Plain and Tall* occurs.

   The illustrations by Garth Williams help to set the time period around the middle of the last century. Fern is wearing a dress. The room smells of damp plaster, which suggests this is an older home. Avery has an air rifle and a wooden dagger, instead of a plastic gun and a knife. A school bus picks up the children for school.

2. List three places where events occur in the book.

   Answers will vary. Sample answers are provided.

   Events occur in the Arables' kitchen, Mr. Zuckerman's barn, and the County Fair.

3. Give one example of an important event that could happen only at a specific time of year.

   Answers will vary. Sample answers are provided.

   Many events in the story are linked to the season of the year. The County Fair is one example. Fern visiting the barn for long periods of time while school is out is another.

4. How would some of the events in *Charlotte's Web* change if the story were set in colonial America? List some of the events that could not happen.

   Answers will vary. Sample answers are provided.

   Fern could not ride the Ferris wheel with Henry Fussy. Avery would not have an air rifle. A school bus wouldn't pick the children up for school. People could not come in their cars to see Charlotte's web. A loudspeaker would not announce Wilbur's special award.

11.9 Aha! Chapters 1–5

Directions: Use the lines provided to answer these questions about chapters 1–5. Refer to the chapters as you answer them. To answer some of the questions, you will need to make an inference 🔍. (Draw a conclusion based on the clues in the story and what you already know.)

Chapter 1

1. Read the first sentence of this story again. When do these events happen? (page 7)

   They happen during the summer.

🔍 2. Opal says she knows she has done something big. (page 10) Explain what Opal has done and why this is "something big."

   Answers will vary. Sample answers are provided.

   She has told the adults at the grocery store that the big stray dog is actually hers. It is big because it is a lie and because she has committed to take care of an animal without permission from her father.

3. Make an inference about why the manager gives Opal a "hard stare" when she calls the dog Winn-Dixie. (page 10)

   Answers will vary. Sample answers are provided.

   The manager isn't sure whether Opal is telling the truth about the dog being hers and being named Winn-Dixie. He thinks maybe she is making fun of him.

4. What inferences can you draw about Winn-Dixie from Opal's description on page 11? Include the details in the text that support your conclusions.

   Answers will vary. Sample answers are provided.

   He hasn't been cared for very well. He is skinny, so he probably has not had enough to eat. He has bald patches, so maybe he has some kind of skin disease that hasn't been treated. She says he looks like a big piece of old carpet left out in the rain. I think this means he is a dirty stray and doesn't show any signs of having a loving owner.

5. What unusual character trait does Winn-Dixie exhibit?

   He smiles.

Chapter 2

6. Why have Opal and her father moved to Naomi, Florida? (page 13)

   They moved so he could be the new preacher at the Open Arms Baptist Church of Naomi.

7. Opal says it is hard for her to think of her father as "daddy," but she thinks of him as "the preacher." (page 13) What inferences can you draw about their relationship from this information?

   Answers will vary. Sample answers are provided.

   He is not very affectionate or open about his feelings. He is stiff and distant. He focuses a lot on his job and not as much on his daughter.

8. How did Opal get her name? (pages 13–14) What does this reveal about her father?

   Answers will vary. Sample answers are provided.

   Her first name is India, where her father was a missionary. This reveals that Christian service is very important to him. Her middle name, Opal, was his mother's name. This reveals that he loved his mother a lot, even if he is not always good at showing his love.

9. What animal is Opal reminded of when she looks at her father? Why? (page 16)

   She is reminded of a turtle because he stays hidden, thinking about things but not really engaging the world around him.

10. What does Opal mean when she says Winn-Dixie was making the preacher "poke his head out of his shell"? (page 18)

    Answers will vary. Sample answers are provided.

    She means that Winn-Dixie is making the preacher stop working and take time to talk.

Chapter 3

11. How does Opal communicate with Winn-Dixie?

    She talks to him.

12. What character traits would you use to describe Opal so far?

    Opal seems spontaneous, friendly, loving, observant, and caring.

13. What character traits would you use to describe Opal's father so far?

    The preacher seems serious, distracted, compassionate, and sad.

14. Why do you think that Opal's father has not told her much about her mother before?

    Answers will vary. Sample answers are provided.

    I think that maybe it makes him sad to talk about her. Maybe he thinks it will also make Opal sad to hear about her.

Chapter 4

15. List two ways in which Opal is similar to her mother. (pages 26–27)

    She has red hair and freckles. She is a fast runner.

16. What does Opal do as soon as her father finishes giving her the information about her mother? (pages 29–30)

    She goes to her room, writes the ten things down, and memorizes them.

Chapter 5

17. Why does Opal understand how Winn-Dixie feels about getting left behind? (page 32)

    She understands because her mother left her behind.

18. List three unusual characteristics about the Open Arms Baptist Church of Naomi. (pages 32–35)

    The building used to be a convenience store, and there are tiles on the floor that spell out "PICK PICK PICK QUICK QUICK QUICK." People have to bring their own chairs. There are mice in the church.

19. What do Opal's prayers reveal about her feelings? (pages 38–39)

    They reveal that she misses her mom a lot and really wants to see her again. They also reveal that she is lonely and wishes she had friends. And they show that she is tenderhearted even toward a mouse.

11.10 The Plot of *Because of Winn-Dixie*

Directions: Answer the questions about the plot thus far on the lines provided.

1. Describe the inciting incident. Why do you think Kate DiCamillo decides to open her book with this event?

   Answers will vary. Sample answers are provided.

The inciting incident happens when Opal meets Winn-Dixie and tells the grocery store manager that he is hers. I think Kate DiCamillo starts with this to show what Opal is like and because Winn-Dixie plays an important role in the book.

2. List some of the background information about Opal and her father that is revealed in these opening chapters.

   We learn that Opal and her father have recently moved to Naomi from Watley in North Florida. We also learn that Opal's mother left when Opal was three. We learn that the preacher was once a missionary in India. Kate DiCamillo reveals this information by having Opal talk directly to the reader and also by having her say things to Winn-Dixie.

3. What is the main problem facing Opal? How is this different from the main problem facing the Wittings? How is it similar?

   The main problem facing Opal is that she is lonely and she misses her mother. It is different because Opal has just moved and the Wittings did not. Opal's mother left, but the Wittings' mother died. It is similar because both Opal and the Witting children are dealing with sadness over the loss of their mothers.

4. Describe some of the ways Kate DiCamillo keeps the rising action rising in chapters 4 and 5.

   She keeps the action rising by revealing more about Opal's mother through the ten things the preacher shares. DiCamillo also continues to show how much Opal misses her by the way Opal immediately writes them down and memorizes them. DiCamillo also shows Opal praying for her mother to come back and telling God about being lonely. All of these things help the reader care more about Opal and her loneliness.

11.11 Setting: *Because of Winn-Dixie*

Directions: List some of the details about where and when the events occur in the story so far. Use the chart in **11.3 Setting: Where and When** to help you.

Details That Show When and Where the Story Occurs	
Details That Show When the Action Occurs	**Details That Show Where the Action Occurs**
Opal is buying a box of macaroni and cheese.	There is a Winn-Dixie grocery store, which is a Southern chain.
The first sentence says "last summer."	The narrator says she lives in Naomi, Florida.
The preacher refers to a car and a microscope, which are modern-day things.	There are scenes at a grocery store, a trailer park, and a church.
	Opal is able to walk places by herself.
	Opal says things like "I brushed him good" and "I worked real hard" that sound Southern.

11.12 Figures of Speech: I Spy Metaphors and Similes

Directions: Answer the questions about some of the metaphors and similes Kate DiCamillo uses in the opening chapters of *Because of Winn-Dixie*. You may need to look at the context in your book to figure out what the unfamiliar object is.

Answers about connotations will vary. Sample answers are provided.

1. Mostly, he looked like a big piece of old brown carpet that had been left out in the rain. (page 11)

Q. What is the unfamiliar object in the sentence above?

A. Winn-Dixie.

Q. What is the unfamiliar object compared to?

A. A big piece of old brown carpet that had been left out in the rain.

Q. What kinds of connotations are created by this simile?

A. It has negative connotations because it makes me think that Winn-Dixie looks worn out and smelly. No one would want to cuddle or be close to a piece of carpet that had been left out in the rain!

2. Sometimes he reminded me of a turtle hiding inside its shell. . . . (page 16)

Q. What is the unfamiliar object in the sentence above?

A. The preacher, Opal's father.

Q. What is the unfamiliar object compared to?

A. A turtle hiding in its shell.

Q. What kinds of connotations are created by this metaphor?

A. It has negative connotations. A turtle hiding in its shell is scared and shy and hard to get to know.

3. "She said it made her feel like a bug under a microscope." (page 28)

Q. What is the unfamiliar experience in the sentence above?

A. Being a preacher's wife.

Q. What is the unfamiliar experience compared to?

A. Being a bug under a microscope.

Q. What kinds of connotations are created by this simile?

A. It has negative connotations. It makes me think of being trapped and examined very closely.

11.14 Setting Affects the Plot

Directions: What does the setting allow Opal to do? Look at the two examples on the next page and then come up with three ideas of your own. You can include characters other than Opal.

- Opal can walk all over town.
- Opal can leave Winn-Dixie outside church.

Answers will vary. Sample answers are provided.

Opal can wash Winn-Dixie in the space outside the trailer.

It is safe enough that Opal can go to the grocery store by herself.

Opal can go to her own room to write down ten facts about her mother.

What does the setting prevent Opal from doing? Look at the two examples below and then come up with three ideas of your own. You can include characters other than Opal.

- Opal cannot play in her own backyard because she and the preacher live in a trailer park.
- Opal cannot be loud or misbehave because Friendly Corners Trailer Park is full of adults.

Answers will vary. Sample answers are provided.

Opal cannot play with her old friends because she has moved away.

Opal cannot ride a subway.

Opal cannot go skiing.

11.15 Read *Because of Winn-Dixie*: Chapters 6–10

Directions: Read chapters 6–10 of *Because of Winn-Dixie*. On the chart below, list three characters you meet in these chapters. Identify the place where Opal meets each one, and list a few descriptive details about each place.

Meet New Characters		
New Character	**Where Opal Meets This Character**	**Details about the Place**
Miss Franny Block	Herman W. Block Memorial Library	It is small and old. It is not fancy. It has a window that Winn-Dixie can see into. It has books on shelves and a desk.
Otis	Gertrude's Pets	There are fish, snakes, mice, lizards, gerbils, and pet supplies. There is a sign on the window that says "No Dogs Allowed." There is a parrot named Gertrude that screams. The pet store is dirty and needs to be swept.
Gloria Dump	Gloria's house	There is a fence with a gate around it. The yard is like a jungle with flowers, vegetables, trees, and vines.

11.17 Aha! Chapters 6–10

Directions: Use the lines provided to answer these questions about chapters 6–10. Refer to the chapters as you answer them. To answer some of the questions, you will need to make an inference 🔍 . (Draw a conclusion based on the clues in the story and what you already know.)

Chapter 6

1. What descriptive details about Miss Franny Block does Kate DiCamillo provide in this chapter?

   She is very small and very old, and she has short gray hair. She weighs hardly anything at all.

2. What event leads to Miss Franny becoming Opal's first friend in Naomi?

   Miss Franny sees Winn-Dixie looking into the window and thinks he is a bear. She screams and hides behinds her desk. This leads to her telling Opal a story and the two of them becoming friends.

3. What two reasons does Opal give to convince Miss Franny to let Winn-Dixie come inside? (page 43)

   She says that he gets lonely without her and that he will be good since he goes to church.

4. What does Opal mean when she says Winn-Dixie has a "large heart"? Is this a literal or figurative statement? (page 44)

   Answers will vary. Sample answers are provided.

   She means he is loving. It is a figurative statement.

Chapter 7

5. Make at least two inferences about Miss Franny's character based on her request for a library for her birthday. (page 46)

   Answers will vary. Sample answers are provided.

   She is confident that her father will want to be generous toward her, and she enjoys sharing with others. Her father had told her she could have anything at all, so she asked for "a whole library." She says that she wanted to share the books.

6. What additional inferences can you make about Miss Franny's character based on the story she tells Opal? Include the details in the book that you use to make the inferences.

   Answers will vary. Sample answers are provided.

   When she was a little girl, she was a know-it-all. I know this because she calls herself "a little-miss-know-it-all" and "a miss-smarty-pants." She loved to read. I know this because her nose was stuck in a book, and she didn't look up when a shadow crossed her desk. She was brave. I know this because she decided that if the bear wanted to eat her, she was going to fight, and then she threw her book at it. Now she is lonely. I know this because she says that all of her friends have died. She is happy about the idea of being friends with Opal and Winn-Dixie. She has a sense of humor because of the way she winks at Opal about Amanda Wilkinson.

7. Why do you think Opal wants to be friends with Miss Franny?

   Answers will vary. Sample answers are provided.

   Opal is lonely and can tell that Miss Franny is lonely too. She knows they both need a friend. She appreciates that Miss Franny would take time to tell her a story. She admires Miss Franny for being brave, and she appreciates that Miss Franny likes Winn-Dixie and lets him come in the library.

8. What character traits would you use to describe Amanda Wilkinson? Include the details in the text that you use to make your inferences. (page 51)

   Answers will vary. Sample answers are provided.

   She is prideful; she wanted to make sure the librarian knew she was an advanced reader. She is also picky about rules; she drew attention to the fact that dogs are not usually allowed in libraries.

Chapter 8

9. Why does Opal decide to go to Gertrude's Pets? Why do you think Opal wants to purchase these items? (page 52)

   Answers will vary. Sample answers are provided.

   She wants to buy a collar and a leash. I think she wants to buy these for Winn-Dixie so that people will know he belongs to somebody.

10. How does Opal know that Winn-Dixie likes what she picks out for him? (page 53)

    He smiles, sneezes, and wags his tail.

11. What problem does Opal have with her decision? What is her solution? (pages 53–54)

    She does not have enough money. She suggests an installment plan or working for Otis.

12. What does Opal say Winn-Dixie is better at than anyone she knows? (page 57)

    She says he is better at making friends than anyone she knows.

13. Why are Sweetie Pie Thomas's eyes "all big and round" when Opal bumps into her? (page 57)

    Answers will vary. Sample answers are provided.

    They are big and round because she saw Gertrude land on Winn-Dixie's head. She is amazed by Winn-Dixie and would like a dog just like him.

14. Explain how things are changing for Opal. What are some reasons Opal gives for why she feels happy? (page 59)

    She is starting to feel at home in Naomi. She says she is happy because she has a dog, a job, Miss Franny Block for a friend, and an invitation to a party.

Chapter 9

15. Why do you think the Dewberry boys think Miss Dump is a witch who eats dogs? (pages 61–63)

    Answers will vary. Sample answers are provided.

    It is probably a rumor that the neighborhood kids have spread around. Kids like to tell stories that are scary and exciting, even if they are not sure if they are true.

16. What metaphor describes Miss Dump's yard? Why? (pages 61 and 63)

    Answers will vary. Sample answers are provided.

    It is like a jungle because it is full of flowers, vegetable, trees, and vines, and it is overgrown.

17. What do you think Gloria Dump means when she says, "I can't see nothing but the general shape of things, so I got to rely on my heart"? (pages 65–66)

Answers will vary. Sample answers are provided.

She is saying that since she is almost blind, she can't base her opinions on outward things. She has to rely on how she feels about people to know them.

18. What reasons does Opal give for telling Gloria Dump her life story? (page 66)

Opal told her story because Winn-Dixie liked Gloria Dump, because the sandwich had tasted so good, and because she had been waiting for a long time to tell someone everything about herself.

Chapter 10

19. What simile does Opal continue to use to describe her father? What do you think her father does that makes her see this resemblance? (page 67)

She says he is like a turtle hiding in his shell. He doesn't share very much about what he thinks or feels. He doesn't put an effort into getting to know Opal or making friends.

20. What does Gloria Dump do while Opal tells her story? Why do you think Opal says "it felt good"? (page 68)

She is nodding, smiling, frowning, and saying things that show she is listening. It feels good because Opal can tell she is listening with all her heart. It feels good to have someone care enough to really pay attention to what you are saying.

21. How does Gloria think Opal might be like her mother (pages 68–69)? What do they do together to test this idea?

She thinks that maybe Opal is good at making things grow too. They test it by planting a tree together.

22. What simile describes planting the tree? (page 69)

    She says it is like tucking a baby into bed.

23. What amazes Opal on page 71? Why?

    Answers will vary. Sample answers are provided.

    She is amazed that the preacher laughs back at Winn-Dixie. She is amazed because she expects him to be angry about Winn-Dixie getting on the bed. He does not laugh often, and he was not excited about Winn-Dixie at first, so his laughing is very surprising to Opal.

11.18 Figures of Speech: Hyperbole

Directions: Read each of the sentences from *Because of Winn-Dixie* below. Explain the point that the hyperbole is emphasizing in each sentence.

1. "She could stick a tire in the ground and grow a car." (page 26)

   The hyperbole emphasizes that Opal's mother was very good at growing things.

2. "She burned everything, including water." (page 27)

   The hyperbole emphasizes that Opal's mother is bad at cooking.

3. "She couldn't make head nor tail of a piece of meat." (page 27)

   The hyperbole makes the point that Opal's mother didn't know much about cooking.

4. "Back when Florida was wild, when it consisted of nothing but palmetto trees and mosquitoes so big they could fly away with you . . ." (page 45)

   The hyperbole emphasizes that the mosquitos were very large.

MODULE 12

12.1 Setting Reveals Character: Part 1

Directions: List three other inferences you can make about snow leopards based on the description of their habitat.

Answers will vary. Sample answers are provided.

Snow leopards hunt mountain goats.

Snow leopards have very thick coats to protect them from the cold.

Snow leopards use the mountainous rocks and cliffs to blend in with their surroundings.

Directions: List three inferences someone could make about you just from looking around your bedroom.

Answers will vary. Sample answers are provided.

Someone could infer that I love horses. Someone could infer that I don't care about neatness. Someone could infer that I love baseball and that the Red Sox are my favorite baseball team.

Directions: Identify the place where you meet each character. Based on the details in the book and your own prior knowledge, what inferences can you draw about these characters from studying their surroundings? Write your answers on the chart on the next page.

The Characters' Natural Habitat		
Character	**Location**	**Inferences**
Miss Franny Block	The Herman W. Block Memorial Library	Miss Franny loves to read.
Otis	Gertrude's Pets	Otis loves animals.

The Characters' Natural Habitat		
Character	**Location**	**Inferences**
Dunlap and Stevie Dewberry	outside their house	They may not have friends other than each other. They may not be allowed to roam around town the way that Opal does.
Gloria Dump	her house	Gloria likes to grow things.

12.2 Read *Because of Winn-Dixie*: Chapters 11–14

Directions: Read chapters 11–14 of *Because of Winn-Dixie*. On the lines below, list new things you learn about each character Opal interacts with.

This list includes some of the new things readers learn about the characters through Opal's interactions with them.

- Winn-Dixie is afraid of thunderstorms.
- The preacher's reaction to Winn-Dixie's fear shows that he is calm and kind in a difficult situation.
- The preacher's handling of the situation shows Opal that he loves Winn-Dixie too.
- Otis can play guitar and sing.
- Otis's music is very important to him.
- Otis's music has a strange effect on animals.
- Otis feels sorry for the animals when they are locked in their cages. He likes to let them out.
- Otis was in prison.
- Sweetie Pie thinks Otis is magical.

- Stevie Dewberry continues to taunt Opal and make her angry.
- Dunlap Dewberry defends Opal. He is not as mean as Stevie.
- Gloria Dump doesn't get mad at the Dewberry boys for what they say about her. She recognizes that they are trying to make friends with Opal.
- Gloria Dump is losing her eyesight.
- Gloria Dump is an alcoholic, but she doesn't drink anymore. She has done things she is ashamed of.
- Because of her past, Gloria doesn't judge people by what they have done. She gives people the benefit of the doubt.

12.4 Aha! Chapters 11–14

Directions: Use the lines provided to answer these questions about chapters 11–14. Refer to the chapters as you answer them. To answer some of the questions, you will need to make an inference 🔍. (Draw a conclusion based on the clues in the story and what you already know.)

Chapter 11

1. How does the weather become a part of the story in chapter 11?

   In chapter 11 we find out that Winn-Dixie has a pathological fear of thunderstorms. The preacher tells Opal that Florida has a lot of thunderstorms during the summer.

2. What simile describes Winn-Dixie charging toward the preacher? (page 74)

   She says that Winn-Dixie charges at the preacher "like he was a bowling ball and the preacher was the only pin left standing."

3. What is a pathological fear? (page 75)

   It is a fear beyond a normal fear. You can't be talked out of it.

4. Can you find a hyperbole that describes Winn-Dixie's reaction? (page 76)

Winn-Dixie is running "to save his life." Winn-Dixie acts "like it was surely the end of the world."

5. How does the problem get more complicated in chapter 11? What possible future event is foreshadowed?

Answers will vary. Sample answers are provided.

We learn that Winn-Dixie is afraid of thunderstorms and that there are a lot of them in Florida. The preacher says they will have to make sure to keep Winn-Dixie inside during a storm so he doesn't run away. Perhaps Winn-Dixie will be left out in a storm and run away later in the story.

Chapter 12

6. What kind of effect does Otis's music have on the animals? (pages 79–81) List some of the figurative language that describes this effect. (page 81)

It makes them become totally still. Opal says that the animals are sitting so still, it was "like they had turned to stone." She also says that when the music stops, it is as if a "spell was broken."

7. Why does Otis like to take the animals out of their cages? (pages 82–83) What does this tell you about his character?

Answers will vary. Sample answers are provided.

Otis takes them out of their cages because he feels sorry for them being locked up all the time. This shows that Otis empathizes with how he thinks the animals must feel.

8. Opal says Otis looked up at her "real quick and then looked back down at his boots." (page 83) Why? What inference can you make about how Otis is feeling at that moment?

Answers will vary. Sample answers are provided.

He feels ashamed. He doesn't want to see how Opal reacts to the news that he has been in jail.

9. What does Opal think her father's reaction to Otis would be? (page 84) Why?

   Answers will vary. Sample answers are provided.

   Opal thinks her father won't want her to work for a criminal. He may think Otis is dangerous or not trustworthy.

10. What is Opal collecting for her mama? (page 85) Why?

   Opal is collecting stories for her mama. She thinks the stories about the people she has met in Naomi will make her laugh.

Chapter 13

11. Where is Opal's favorite place to be this summer? (page 88)

   Her favorite place is Gloria Dump's yard.

12. Why doesn't Opal get along with the Dewberry boys? (pages 89–90)

   They still believe Gloria Dump is a witch even though Opal tells them this isn't true. Stevie repeats things that his mother has said about Opal, like that she shouldn't spend all her time indoors talking to old ladies. He also says unkind things about Otis.

13. What simile describes Opal's daily encounters with the Dewberry brothers? (page 90)

   She says that she "felt like a soldier who had been fighting a hard battle."

14. Why do you think Gloria isn't upset that the boys call her names? What does she think the Dewberry brothers are trying to do? (page 91)

   Answers will vary. Sample answers are provided.

   She is old enough to understand that the boys are just trying to get Opal's attention. She thinks they are trying to make friends with Opal.

Chapter 14

15. What does Gloria show Opal when Opal tells her that Otis has been in jail? (pages 93–95)

    She shows Opal a tree with a lot of empty alcohol bottles tied to it.

16. What does the tree represent to Gloria? (page 95)

    She tells Opal that the tree represents the "ghost of all the things I done wrong."

17. What does Gloria say is the most important thing she has learned in life? (page 96)

    You can't judge people by the things they've done. You have to judge them by the things they are doing now.

18. What does Opal wonder about when she looks at Gloria's tree? (page 97)

    She wonders if her mother has a tree full of bottles like Gloria's. She wonders if she is like a ghost to her mother the way her mother can seem like a ghost to her.

12.5 Setting: Reveals Character: Part 2

Directions: Now you try. Choose two different settings from the list on the next page. Using details from the book and your own prior knowledge, make inferences about the similarities and differences between the two settings. (Do not choose both Gloria Dump's House and Gertrude's Pets.) Then answer the questions.

Answers will vary. Sample answers are provided.

Settings:

Friendly Corners Trailer Park
Open Arms Baptist Church
Gertrude's Pets
Henry W. Block Memorial Library
Gloria Dump's house

Choose two settings from the story:

1. How are these settings alike? List your answers on the Venn diagram.

   Open Arms Baptist Church/Friendly Corners Trailer Park: Both have space for many people. Both are a community. Both probably have mice.

   Open Arms Baptist Church/Gertrude's Pets: Both have mice. There is music in both places.

   Open Arms Baptist Church/Henry W. Block Memorial Library: Both have books. (The church probably has Bibles and hymnals.)

   Open Arms Baptist Church/Gloria Dump's house: Both welcome visitors and new people. Both have good things to eat.

   Gertrude's Pets/Friendly Corners Trailer Park: Both have pets.

   Gertrude's Pets/Henry W. Block Memorial Library: Dogs are not allowed in either place, but an exception is made for Winn-Dixie.

   Henry W. Block Memorial Library/Friendly Corners Trailer Park: Both may have books. In both places, people are supposed to be quiet.

   Henry W. Block Memorial Library/Gloria Dump's house: Both are houses. Both have women in charge who like to tell stories.

   Gloria Dump's house/Friendly Corners Trailer Park: Both places are usually quiet.

2. How are these settings different? List your answers on the Venn diagram.

   Open Arms Baptist Church/Friendly Corners Trailer Park: Children are allowed to attend the church. Only adults are supposed to live in the trailer park.

   Open Arms Baptist Church/Gertrude's Pets: People go to the church to sing hymns and listen to a sermon. People go to Gertrude's Pets to shop.

   Open Arms Baptist Church/Henry W. Block Memorial Library: People can talk and sing at the church. They have to be quiet at the library.

   Open Arms Baptist Church/Gloria Dump's house: The Baptist church meets in an old grocery store. Gloria's house is overgrown with plants.

Gertrude's Pets/Friendly Corners Trailer Park: People can live at the trailer park. Only animals live at the pet store.

Gertrude's Pets/Henry W. Block Memorial Library: One is filled with animals. The other is filled with books.

Henry W. Block Memorial Library/Friendly Corners Trailer Park: The library doesn't have any trailers. It is in a house.

Henry W. Block Memorial Library/Gloria Dump's house: Gloria's house has a large garden. The library does not.

Gloria Dump's house/Friendly Corners Trailer Park: Opal and Winn-Dixie have to be quiet at the trailer park. They don't have to be quiet at Gloria's house.

3. What does each setting tell you about the characters you find there?

Answers will vary. Sample answers are provided.

Friendly Corners Trailer Park: The preacher can't afford a house.

Open Arms Baptist Church: The people who attend don't mind holding church in a casual setting.

Library: Miss Franny loves to read.

Gertrude's Pets: Otis is more comfortable around animals than people.

Gloria Dump's house: Gloria loves growing things.

12.6 Plot: Episodic Structure

Directions: Reread chapters 5 and 11. Then use the chart on the next page to show how each chapter is a self-contained story, like an episode of a television show. Describe the events in each chapter that make up the inciting incident, rising action, climax, and falling action. An example based on chapter 1 shows you how to complete this activity.

Episodic Plots in *Because of Winn-Dixie*

	Chapter 5 Event	Chapter 11 Event
Inciting Incident	The preacher ties up Winn-Dixie outside the church. When he starts preaching, Winn-Dixie starts to howl until the preacher lets Opal bring him inside.	A thunderstorm begins.
Rising Action	A mouse runs across the floor. Winn-Dixie chases the mouse. Winn-Dixie catches the mouse.	Winn-Dixie whines to be let out of Opal's room. Winn-Dixie darts to the preacher's room and wakes him up. The thunderstorm gets worse. Winn-Dixie goes crazy with fear in the trailer. He runs wildly everywhere. The preacher explains to Opal that Winn-Dixie must have a pathological fear of storms.
Climax	Winn-Dixie brings the mouse to the preacher. Everyone gets real quiet. The preacher says, "Let us pray for this mouse." Everyone laughs and claps.	The storm finally stops. Winn-Dixie stops running around.
Falling Action	The preacher tosses the mouse out the front door. Opal prays about her loneliness.	Winn-Dixie climbs on the couch with Opal and her daddy. The preacher tells Opal they will have to make sure Winn-Dixie doesn't get out in a storm and run away.
Resolution	Opal prays for the mouse.	Opal thinks about how much she loves the preacher.

12.7 Figures of Speech: I Spy Similes

Directions: Now look at some examples of similes from *Because of Winn-Dixie* on the next page. Underline the simile in each sentence. Circle the word or words that signal the beginning of the simile. Think about what the simile is communicating. Then rewrite each sentence creating a new simile to replace the one you underlined in the original sentence. Try to keep the meaning and emotions similar to the original simile, but use a different comparison.

Answers will vary. Sample answers are provided.

1. . . . Winn-Dixie looked like a furry bullet, shooting across the building, chasing that mouse. (page 36)

   New simile: **Winn-Dixie looked like a rocket, shooting across the building, chasing that mouse.**

2. I told her about the preacher being like a turtle, hiding all the time inside his shell. (page 67)

   New simile: **I told her about the preacher being like a hermit crab, scuttling back into the sea.**

3. I swear, it about wore me out yelling at Dunlap and Stevie Dewberry every day; by the time I got to Gloria Dump's yard, I felt like a soldier who had been fighting a hard battle. (page 90)

   New simile: **By the time I got to Gloria Dump's yard, I felt like a runner who had just finished a marathon.**

4. Some of his fur was pretty loose and blew right off of him like a dandelion puff. (page 98)

   New simile: **Some of his fur was pretty loose and blew right off him like confetti.**

Directions: Create your own similes from the sentences below by adding a comparison and using the signal words *like* or *as*. When you have finished, discuss your answers with a parent, teacher, or reading coach.

1. Miss Franny sat there trembling and shaking. (page 42)

   New simile: Miss Franny sat there trembling and shaking like a house in an earthquake.

2. "He has a large heart, too." (page 44)

   New simile: He has a heart as large as an ocean.

3. He sat up then and showed Miss Franny his teeth. (page 50)

   New simile: He sat up then and showed Miss Franny his teeth, bared like he was doing a toothpaste commercial.

12.8 Read *Because of Winn-Dixie*: Chapters 15–19

Directions: On the chart on the next page, list what each character is reminded of after eating a Littmus Lozenge. Make an inference about each character based on his or her reaction to the lozenge.

Answers will vary. Sample answers are provided.

Littmus Lozenge Inferences		
Character	**Littmus Lozenge Tastes Like/ Reminds Of**	**An Inference I Can Make about This Character**
Amanda	It makes her think of things she feels sad about. It makes her miss Carson.	Something very sad has happened to Amanda. It probably has something to do with someone named Carson.
Gloria	It tastes sweet. It tastes like people leaving.	People she cares about have left her sometime in the past.
the preacher	He says it tastes a little melancholy. It makes him think of Opal's mother.	The preacher feels melancholy a lot. Maybe he doesn't talk about Opal's mother because he feels too sad to talk about her.

Littmus Lozenge Inferences		
Character	**Littmus Lozenge Tastes Like/ Reminds Of**	**An Inference I Can Make about This Character**
Otis	He says it tastes good but also a little bit like jail.	Jail was a very difficult experience for Otis. It has made him the way he is now.
Sweetie Pie	She said it tasted like not having a dog.	Sweetie Pie really wants to have a dog of her own.

What do you think the Littmus Lozenge would remind you of if you tasted it? Why?

Answers will vary.

12.10 Aha! Chapters 15–19

Directions: Use the lines provided to answer these questions about chapters 15–19. Refer to the chapters as you answer them. To answer some of the questions, you will need to make an inference . (Draw a conclusion based on the clues in the story and what you already know.)

Chapter 15

1. Why does Opal hold on to Winn-Dixie during thunderstorms? (page 100) Does this action resolve the problem?

   She doesn't want him to run away. It is working so far.

2. Why does Opal decide to read Gloria Dump a book? (page 100)

   She decides to read to Gloria because she wants to comfort Gloria when she thinks about the things she has done wrong. She has bad eyesight and can't read anymore.

Chapter 16

3. What did Littmus W. Block find when he finished fighting in the Civil War? (pages 107–108)

   His house had been burned to the ground. His mother and sisters had died of typhoid fever. His father had been killed in the war.

4. Opal says, "It was important to me to hear how Littmus survived after losing everything he loved." (page 109) Why do you think this is important to Opal?

   Answers will vary. Sample answers are provided.

   It is important to her because she has lost someone she loves and she wants to know how to survive this.

Chapter 17

5. What does "he missed the boy he used to be" mean? (page 110)

   Answers will vary. Sample answers are provided.

   War has changed Littmus. He wishes he could be carefree and happy like he was when he was a boy.

6. Why do you think Opal wants to share the Littmus Lozenge with all of her new friends?

   Answers will vary. Sample answers are provided.

   She probably knows they have sadness in their lives, and they will find something comforting in the Littmus Lozenge just like she has.

7. What details do you notice in chapter 17 that show Opal is changing? Why do you think she is changing?

   Answers will vary. Sample answers are provided.

   She decides to wave at the Dewberry boys when she rides past instead of ignoring them. She also thinks about Amanda and how neat it is that she also enjoys a good story. She wonders about who Carson is because she is starting to care about Amanda. She is changing because Miss Franny and Gloria are helping her to think about how other people might feel. She is realizing that many people have sorrows in their lives and need friends.

Chapter 18

8. What words of wisdom does the preacher give Opal (page 125)

   "Other people's tragedies should not be the subject of idle conversation."

9. What does Opal think about when her father tucks her into bed? (pages 126–127)

   She thinks about how life is like a Littmus Lozenge, with sweet and sad both mixed up together. She thinks about the word "melancholy." And she thinks about Amanda and her brother Carson, who won't have a sixth birthday party.

Chapter 19

10. What do Opal and Otis have in common? (page 130)

    Answers will vary. Sample answers are provided.

    They are both lonely.

11. What is different about Sweetie Pie's reaction to the lozenge? Why do you think that her reaction is different from the others'? (page 132)

    Answers will vary. Sample answers are provided.

    She spits out the candy and she doesn't like the taste of it. She hasn't learned that sorrow is something that can be savored along with sweetness.

MODULE 13

13.1 The Story So Far

Directions: Answer the questions about *Because of Winn-Dixie* using details from the book. Discuss your answers with a parent, teacher, or reading coach.

1. Who is the main character in this story? Give three reasons to support your choice.

   Opal is the main character. Opal is the narrator, so we get to know her better than any other character. Opal is most affected by the action in the story. Finding Winn-Dixie changes her life more than any other character's life. The action revolves around Opal. She is in every scene in the book.

2. What information does the author provide about the main character's life before the events in this story take place?

   We know that Opal used to live in northern Florida. We know that her mother has left her and her father.

3. What is the main conflict facing the main character? Support your choice with details from the story.

   Opal is lonely. She has moved to a new town and doesn't have any friends. Her mother has left her, and Opal doesn't know if she is coming back.

4. What is the inciting incident of this story?

   The inciting incident is when Opal rescues Winn-Dixie in the grocery store. From that event Winn-Dixie becomes hers, and through Winn-Dixie she meets all her new friends.

5. What complications have made the main conflict worse?

   Winn-Dixie is afraid of thunderstorms. Even though Opal makes new friends, she is storing up stories from her new life to share with her mother when she comes back. If her mother doesn't come back, this may make Opal feel even more abandoned.

6. What events so far are making the main conflict better?

   Meeting Winn-Dixie leads to Opal meeting Miss Franny, Gloria Dump, Otis, and others who want to be her friends. Opal is also starting to realize that other people have experienced sadness, and this helps her feel not so alone.

7. What is one thing most of the characters in *Because of Winn-Dixie* have in common?

   Answers will vary. Sample answers are provided.

   The characters in the book are all lonely. Something sad has happened to all of them. Even Sweetie Pie is sad about not having a dog.

13.2 Make a Prediction

Directions: In *Because of Winn-Dixie*, Kate DiCamillo uses an element of the setting to complicate Opal's main conflict and foreshadow a possible future event. What is that element? What might it foreshadow? Write your answer below. If you need help, look on page 72 of the novel.

The element of setting that complicates the central conflict is the weather. A thunderstorm occurs. Opal and the preacher find out that Winn-Dixie has a pathological fear of thunderstorms. The preacher tells Opal they will have to make sure that Winn-Dixie doesn't get out in a thunderstorm because he might run away. A thunderstorm might occur later in the story. Perhaps Winn-Dixie will get out and run away.

13.3 Read *Because of Winn-Dixie*: Chapters 20–22

Directions: Read chapters 20–22 of *Because of Winn-Dixie*. As you read, list the events in this section that add anticipation or tension to the story on the lines below.

Answers will vary. Sample answers are provided.

Opal decides to have a party, and she wants it to be "the best party ever."

Gloria insists that she invite the Dewberry boys to it. Miss Franny encourages Opal to invite Amanda. Amanda agrees to come. Otis doesn't want to come at first, but Opal promises free cleaning if he does. He comes, but he is very uncomfortable. At the end of chapter 22, thunder is heard in the distance, and it starts to rain.

13.5 Aha! Chapters 20–22

Directions: Use the lines provided to answer these questions about chapters 20–22. Refer to the chapters as you answer them. To answer some of the questions, you will need to make an inference. (Draw a conclusion based on the clues in the story and what you already know.)

Chapter 20

1. Why does Gloria Dump laugh when she finds out why Otis was in jail? (pages 133–134)

   Answers will vary. Sample answers are provided.

   She thinks it is silly that they locked him up for playing his guitar. She tells Opal that sometimes things are so sad they are funny.

2. How does Gloria respond when Opal asks her, "Do you think everybody misses somebody?" (page 134)

   Gloria says she thinks so. She says sometimes she thinks "that the whole world has an aching heart."

3. Why do you think Opal wants to have a party? Use details from the story to support your answer. (page 136)

   Answers will vary. Sample answers are provided.

   I think she thinks a party will cheer up everyone who is sad. It will also give Otis a chance to play his guitar for people.

4. What will this event allow Opal to do for the first time since meeting her new friends in Naomi?

It will allow Opal to introduce her new friends to each other.

5. Why do you think Gloria wants Opal to invite the Dewberry boys? (pages 137–138)

Answers will vary. Sample answers are provided.

She knows they are also lonely. She knows they are trying to make friends with Opal. Perhaps she wants to show them that she is not a witch.

6. Whom does Miss Franny Block encourage Opal to invite? Why? (page 139)

Answers will vary. Sample answers are provided.

She wants Opal to invite Amanda. She thinks Amanda and Opal could become friends. She probably also thinks the party will help to cheer up Amanda.

7. How does Otis feel about coming to the party? What evidence in the book helps you to know how he feels? (pages 141–142)

Answers will vary. Sample answers are provided.

He is nervous about coming to a party, but he is secretly glad he is invited. At first he says no, but then he agrees to come when Opal says he will not have to talk to anyone. He smiles when he looks down at his boots.

Chapter 21

8. Notice the metaphors and similes Kate DiCamillo uses in chapter 21. Write down the comparisons used to describe each of the following:

Gloria's backyard (page 145)

She compares Gloria's backyard to a fairyland.

Miss Franny Block (page 145)

She uses a simile to compare how Miss Franny Block stands in her heels to someone standing in a boat.

Otis (page 149)

She says Otis looks like he is lost. She says that Opal talks to him like she is trying to get a wild animal to take food out of her hand.

Chapter 22

9. How does Kate DiCamillo show readers that Otis is uncomfortable when he first arrives at the party? List some of the clues she provides. (pages 150–152)

   Otis doesn't know what to do when the preacher offers to shake his hand. He doesn't know what to do with the big jar of pickles. When he sets it on the ground, his guitar hits him in the head. He wipes his hands on his pants because they are probably sweating from his nervousness. He tells the preacher that he has brought pickles, which everyone can see. On page 152, Opal says that Otis's face is red.

10. What happens at the end of chapter 22? Predict what you think might happen next in the story. (page 154)

    Answers will vary. Sample answers are provided.

    Thunder is heard in the distance, and then it starts to rain. A thunderstorm will probably happen next.

13.6 Figures of Speech: Personification

Directions: Why do you think an author might use personification? How does this figure of speech improve a story? (You might try thinking through how the story would change if Kate DiCamillo didn't use personification to describe Winn-Dixie.) Write your best ideas on the lines below. Discuss your answers with a parent, teacher, or reading coach.

Answers will vary. Sample answers are provided.

Giving animals human characteristics helps us to view them the same way we view a person. Personification helps us to have empathy for the animals.

13.7 Character Development: Is Winn-Dixie a Character?

Directions: What makes someone in a story a character? Write your answer to the question using at least three complete sentences below. You can use your own ideas, information you have learned from using *Readers in Residence*, and your background knowledge. You can refer back to the modules about character development in unit 1 to help you.

Answers will vary. Sample answers are provided.

A character in the story appears in the events in the story. A character in a story is affected by the action. A character in the story interacts with other characters. A character in a story has a name.

Directions: Give your best reasons for why you believe Winn-Dixie should or should not be considered a character in this story. There is no right answer, but a good answer will use details from the book to support your position. Discuss your reasons with a parent, teacher, or reading coach.

Answers will vary. Sample answers are provided.

Winn-Dixie is a character:

He has a name.

He can't talk, but you know what he is thinking because he can smile.

Opal talks to him.

He interacts with all the other characters.

He is affected by the action.

Winn-Dixie is not a character:

He doesn't speak like Wilbur and Charlotte do.

Even though Opal acts like she knows what he is thinking, we don't really know what Winn-Dixie thinks.

He is not affected by the main conflict the way the other characters are.

He doesn't have feelings and thoughts the way that the human characters do.

13.9 Read *Because of Winn-Dixie*: Chapters 23–26

Directions: Read chapters 23–26 of *Because of Winn-Dixie*. Fill out the chart on the next page with your best ideas about the plot points.

The Conclusion of *Because of Winn-Dixie*	
Plot Point	**What Happens**
Climax	Winn-Dixie gets lost in the thunderstorm because he is afraid. Opal and her father search for him in the pouring rain. Opal is reunited with Winn-Dixie when she and her father return to Gloria Dump's house.
Turning Point	Opal gets angry with her father. Her father starts to cry. He tells Opal he doesn't think her mother is ever coming back. They hug each other.
Falling Action	Opal learns how her friends found Winn-Dixie. She goes out to Gloria's backyard.
Resolution	They sing songs together and pass Littmus Lozenges around.

13.11 Aha! Chapters 23–26

Directions: Use the lines provided to answer these questions about chapters 23–26. Refer to the chapters as you answer them. To answer some of the questions, you will need to make an inference. (Draw a conclusion based on the clues in the story and what you already know.)

Chapter 23

1. What piece of advice does Gloria Dump give Opal? (page 159) Do you think this advice concerns only Winn-Dixie?

   Answers will vary. Sample answers are provided.

   Gloria tells Opal that you can't hold on to something that wants to go. You can only love what you have while you have it. This advice is about Winn-Dixie, but it probably is also about Opal's mother.

2. Why do you think the sight of Dunlap Dewberry standing on the porch makes Opal feel sad? (page 160)

   Answers will vary. Sample answers are provided.

   It might make Opal sad because she realizes that Dunlap coming to her party shows that he does want to be friends. But now it is raining and Winn-Dixie is lost. She doesn't have time to make friends with him at the party.

Chapter 24

3. Who helps Opal search for Winn-Dixie? (page 161)

   Her father does.

4. Why does Opal make a list of ten things she knows about Winn-Dixie? (page 162) What previous list has she made? (page 163)

   She makes a list of ten things she knows about Winn-Dixie so she can put them on a poster and hang it up around the neighborhood. This list is like the one she made about her mother earlier in the book.

5. Why does making the list of ten things make Opal sadder? (page 164)

   She realizes that listing what you know about someone doesn't begin to show what he or she is really like. She realizes she doesn't really know her mama.

6. Why does Opal get angry with her father while searching for Winn-Dixie? (page 165) What else is she angry about?

   Answers will vary. Sample answers are provided.

   Opal gets angry with her father because he wants to give up on looking for Winn-Dixie. But she is really angry because she thinks he always gives up. She thinks he did not try to prevent her mother from leaving.

7. What important new understanding occurs to Mr. Buloni about what his wife has left behind? (page 167) (You can review his old understanding on page 29.)

   He realizes that his wife has left him with Opal, and he is very grateful for that.

Chapter 25

8. What important change happens to Opal's friends while she is out searching for Winn-Dixie? (page 175)

   They all become friends.

9. Why do you think the preacher asks Otis to play a hymn at the end of this chapter?

   Answers will vary. Sample answers are provided.

   He is grateful to God for everything that has just happened. He thinks it is appropriate to thank God for resolving things with Opal and for their new friends in Naomi.

Chapter 26

10. What important change has happened to Opal over the summer? (page 178)

    Opal feels her heart fill up with happiness. She doesn't feel empty because her mother has left her anymore. She will keep thinking about her mother, but probably not as often as she did that summer.

11. When Opal looks at the tree that she and Gloria Dump planted in the yard, what does she find? (page 178)

    She is surprised by how much it has grown. It still looks more like a plant than a tree. But she can tell that it is bigger and stronger than she expected.

12. What change takes place between Dunlap Dewberry and Opal? (pages 179–180)

    Both Opal and Dunlap realize they were wrong about each other. They realize they want to be friends. Dunlap reaches out his hand to help Opal off the ground, and they race to the house, signaling their new friendship.

13. What do you think Opal means when she says, "and the flavor of the Littmus Lozenge opened in my mouth like a flower blooming, all sweet and sad"? (page 182)

    Answers will vary. Sample answers are provided.

    I think this means that in life the sweet and sad are mixed together. It is hard to sort out what is sweet from what is sad.

13.12 Theme: Something to Think about

Directions: Find the statement in the final chapters of *Because of Winn-Dixie* repeated by two characters. Write it below. Discuss what you think this means with a parent, teacher, or reading coach.

You can't hold on to anything. You can only love what you've got while you've got it. (pages 159 and 167)

13.13 Genre: Why Is *Because of Winn-Dixie* Contemporary Realistic Fiction?

Directions: In the space below, list some details from the book that show you why *Because of Winn-Dixie* should be classified as contemporary realistic fiction.

Answers will vary. Sample answers are provided.

Characters: Give examples of how the major characters in the story have lives similar to yours. Give examples of how the main character matures or grows wiser as a result of the events in the story.

The major characters are children who do things I do. They ride bikes. They enjoy parties. They play outside. The adults live in houses or a trailer park. The kinds of jobs they have are similar to jobs people have today. The main character is Opal. She learns how to make new friends, and she learns how to deal with missing her mother.

Setting: Provide details that show that the story is set in a real place during the current time period. List the names of real places in the story that you can find on a map.

The story takes place in Naomi, Florida. Even though Naomi is not a real small town in Florida, Florida is a real place. Florida does have a lot of thunderstorms, especially in the summer. The stores in the book, like the Winn-Dixie grocery store and Gertrude's Pets, show it is set during a recent time period. The trailer park also indicates a recent time period. The Baptist church meets in an old grocery store. This is also a clue it is a contemporary time period.

Dialogue: Give examples of the things the characters talk about that are similar to things you talk about with your friends and family. Give examples of words and phrases you or people you know use that are unique to this time period.

Opal talks about moving, friendship, loneliness, sadness, her mother leaving, Winn-Dixie, and about Otis and the others she meets. These are all similar to topics I talk about with my friends and family. Opal calls her father "Daddy." In older times, children were more likely to call their father "Papa" or "Father."

Plot: Explain how the events in the story involve problems that have happened or could happen to you or others you know. Show how the main character experiences a significant inward change.

Opal's mother has left. Opal and her father have moved to a new place. She becomes friends with some children she doesn't think she wants to be friends with at first. Her father is distant and sad. Opal learns how to understand her father, and they end up with a better relationship. Some of these things have happened to me. I know some of my friends have had problems like these too.

Conflict: Explain how the main conflict facing the main character involves growing up or fitting in.

Opal's mother has left, and Opal and her father have moved to a new place. Opal is lonely. The central problem is about Opal making new friends and accepting that her mother has left and may never return.

Theme: Explain what you learned from reading this book about yourself or other young people you know or may meet sometime.

I learned that I should be grateful for the friends and pets I have right now. I understand better what it must feel like for someone to have a parent leave. I understood how Opal felt about moving to a new place because I had to move away from all my friends a few years ago.

Suggested Daily Schedule

Week	Day 1	Day 2	Day 3	Day 4
1	**Intro to Unit 1** Read welcome letter. Read Unit 1 Introduction. Study the unit project rubric.	**Module 1** Reader's Questions – 1.7	**Module 1** 1.8 – 1.11	**Module 1** 1.12 – Checklist 1
2	**Module 2** Meet Patricia MacLachlan Reader's Questions – 2.3	**Module 2** 2.4 – 2.6	**Module 2** 2.7	**Module 2** 2.8 – 2.9
3	**Module 2** 2.10	**Module 2** 2.11 – 2.13	**Module 2** 2.14 – Checklist 2	**Module 3** Reader's Questions – 3.3 (Start 3.1)
4	**Module 3** 3.4 – 3.5 (Continue 3.1)	**Module 3** 3.6	**Module 3** 3.7 – 3.8 (Finish 3.1)	**Module 3** 3.9
5	**Module 3** 3.10 – 3.11	**Module 3** 3. 12 – 3.13	**Module 3** 3.14 – 3.16	**Module 3** 3.17
6	**Module 3** 3.18 – 3.19	**Module 3** 3.20 – Checklist 3	**Module 4** Reader's Questions – 4.3	**Module 4** 4.3 – 4.4

Suggested Daily Schedule

Week	Day 1	Day 2	Day 3	Day 4
7	**Module 4** 4.5 – 4.7	**Module 4** 4.8 – 4.10	**Module 4** 4.11	**Module 4** 4.12 – 4.13
8	**Module 4** 4.14	**Module 4** 4.15	**Module 4** 4. 16 Unit Project	**Module 4** 4.16 Unit Project
9	**Module 4** 4.16 Unit Project – 4.16 Rubric	**Module 4** Checklist 4	**Intro to Unit 2** Read Unit 2 Introduction. Pick your book.	**Module 5** 5.1 – 5.4
10	**Module 5** 5.5 – 5.6 Read OYO Book	**Module 5** Read OYO Book – (5.7 – 5.8)	**Module 5** Read OYO Book – (5.7 – 5.8)	**Module 5** Read OYO Book – (5.7 – 5.8)
11	**Module 5** 5. 9 – 5.10	**Module 5** 5.11 – 5.12	**Module 5** 5.13 – 5.14	**Module 5** 5.15 – 5.16
12	**Module 5** 5.17 – 5.18	**Module 5** 5.19 – Checklist 5	**Intro to Unit 3** Read Unit 3 Introduction. Study the unit project rubric.	**Module 6** Reader's Questions – 6.3
13	**Module 6** 6.4 – Meet the Illustrator	**Module 6** 6.5 – 6.7	**Module 6** 6.8 – 6.9	**Module 6** 6.10
14	**Module 6** 6.11 – 6.12	**Module 6** 6.13 – 6.15	**Module 6** 6.16 – 6.17	**Module 6** 6.18 – 6.19

Suggested Daily Schedule

Week	Day 1	Day 2	Day 3	Day 4
15	**Module 6** 6.20 – Checklist 6	**Module 7** Reader's Questions – 7.3	**Module 7** 7.4 – 7.5	**Module 7** 7.6 – 7.9
16	**Module 7** 7.10 – 7.11	**Module 7** 7.12 – 7.14	**Module 7** 7. 15 – Checklist 7	**Module 8** Reader's Questions – 8.3
17	**Module 8** 8.4	**Module 8** 8.5 – 8.7	**Module 8** 8.8 – 8.10	**Module 8** 8.11 – 8.12
18	**Module 8** 8.13 – Checklist 8	**Module 9** Reader's Questions –9.3	**Module 9** 9.4 – 9.6	**Module 9** 9.7
19	**Module 9** 9.8 – 9.10	**Module 9** 9.11	**Module 9** 9.11 – 9.13	**Module 9** 9.14
20	**Module 9** 9.15 Unit Project	**Module 9** 9.15 Unit Project	**Module 9** 9.15 Unit Project	**Module 9** 9.15 Rubric – Checklist 9 **Intro to Unit 4** Read Unit 4 Introduction. Pick your book.
21	**Module 10** 10.1 –10.3	**Module 10** 10.4 –10.6 Read OYO Book	**Module 10** Read OYO Book (10.7 – 10.8)	**Module 10** Read OYO Book (10.7 – 10.8)

Suggested Daily Schedule

Week	Day 1	Day 2	Day 3	Day 4
22	**Module 10** Read OYO Book (10.7 – 10.8)	**Module 10** 10.9 – 10.11	**Module 10** 10.12 –10.13	**Module 10** 10.14 –10.15
23	**Module 10** 10.16	**Module 10** 10.17 – Checklist 10	**Intro to Unit 5** Read Unit 5 Introduction. Study the unit project rubric.	**Module 11** Reader's Questions – 11.2
24	**Module 11** 11.3 – 11.6	**Module 11** 11.7 – 11.8	**Module 11** 11.9	**Module 11** 11. 9 – 11.10
25	**Module 11** 11.11 – 11.12	**Module 11** 11.13 – 11.15	**Module 11** 11.16 – 11.17	**Module 11** 11.17
26	**Module 11** 11.18 – Checklist 11	**Module 12** Reader's Questions – 12.2	**Module 12** 12. 3 – 12.4	**Module 12** 12. 4 – 12.5
27	**Module 12** 12.6 – 12.7	**Module 12** 12.8 – 12.9	**Module 12** 12.10	**Module 12** 12.11 – Checklist 12
28	**Module 13** Reader's Questions – 13.3	**Module 13** 13.4 – 13.5	**Module 13** 13.6 – 13.7	**Module 13** 13.8 – 13.10
29	**Module 13** 13.11	**Module 13** 13.12 – 13.13	**Module 13** 13.14 – 13.15 Unit Project	**Module 13** Unit Project

Suggested Daily Schedule

Week	Day 1	Day 2	Day 3	Day 4
30	**Module 13** Unit Project	**Module 13** 13.15 Rubric – Checklist 13 **Intro to Unit 6** Read Unit 6 Introduction. Pick your book.	**Module 14** 14.1 –14.3	**Module 14** 14.4 – 14.5 Read OYO Book
31	**Module 14** Read OYO Book (14.6 – 14.8)	**Module 14** Read OYO Book (14.6 – 14.8)	**Module 14** Read OYO Book (14.6 – 14.8)	**Module 14** 14.9 – 14.10
32	**Module 14** 14.11 – 14.12	**Module 14** 14. 13	**Module 14** 14.14 – 14.15	**Module 14** 14. 16 – Checklist 14

Book Clubs = 5 days

Book Club 1	Book Club 2	Book Club 3	Book Club 4	Book Club 5

Unit 1 Student Rubric

Rubric Point System:

5 points – This part of the project is outstanding.

4 points – This part of the project is very strong.

3 points – This part of the project shows a lot of effort.

2 points – This part of the project needs improvement.

1 point – This part of the project is missing.

In the appendix of the Student Text and Workbook, you will find Reviewer's Rubric 4.16, which readers can use to give the student feedback on the assignment.

Rubric for Unit 1 Project	
Traits of Good Character Development	Points Earned
Physical Traits • I have described some of my main character's physical traits.	
Character Traits • I have described how I will show what my character is like through what he or she says.	
• I have described how I will show what my character is like through what he or she does.	
• I have described how I will show what my character is like through what others say about him or her.	
Conflict • I have described a significant problem my character faces in the story.	
Response • I have described how my character responds to the significant problem he or she faces.	
Changes • I have described how my character changes because of the significant problem he or she faces.	
• I have described how I will show this change through what my character learns, says, does, or thinks.	

Unit 1 Student Rubric

Rubric for Unit 1 Project	
Traits of Good Character Development	Points Earned
Quality • I have created a complete project with the required elements.	
• I have created a high-quality project. I was careful, thoughtful, and creative.	
Effort • I worked hard on my project, and it reflects an appropriate amount of effort.	
Conventions • I have followed the rules for capitalization and punctuation.	
• I have checked to make sure all my words are spelled correctly.	
Total	

Unit 1 project: 65 points possible

Rubric Point System:

5 points – This part of the project is outstanding.

4 points – This part of the project is very strong.

3 points – This part of the project shows a lot of effort.

2 points – This part of the project needs improvement.

1 point – This part of the project is missing.

Unit 3 Student Rubric

Rubric Point System:

5 points – This part of the project is outstanding.

4 points – This part of the project is very strong.

3 points – This part of the project shows a lot of effort.

2 points – This part of the project needs improvement.

1 point – This part of the project is missing.

In the appendix of the Student Text and Workbook, you will find Reviewer's Rubric 9.15, which readers can use to give the student feedback on the assignment.

Rubric for Unit 3 Project	
Traits of Good Plot Development	Points Earned
Exposition • I have included clues about the time and place of my story in the illustrations of the exposition.	
• I have introduced the major characters in the illustrations of the exposition.	
Inciting Incident • I have created one or more illustrations of an inciting incident that will trigger the rest of the action.	
• The illustration(s) of the inciting incident introduces the conflict (significant problem) that the major characters must resolve.	
Rising Action • I have created several illustrations that show events that make the conflict more complicated.	
• I have shown in my illustrations how the tension and the suspense will increase.	
• I have shown in my illustrations how the rising action affects some of my major characters.	
Climax • I have created one or more illustrations of the climax event.	
• My climax illustrations show how the conflict is resolved.	
Falling Action and Resolution • I have created one or more illustrations that show how all the complications are resolved.	

Unit 3 Student Rubric

Rubric for Unit 3 Project	
Traits of Good Plot Development	Points Earned
• I have shown in one or more illustrations how some of my major characters have matured or changed.	
• I have shown in my final illustration what my major characters' lives are like now.	
Quality • I have created a complete project with the required number of elements.	
• I have created a high-quality project. I was careful, thoughtful, and creative.	
Effort • I worked hard on my project, and it reflects an appropriate amount of effort.	
Conventions • I have followed the rules for capitalization and punctuation.	
• I have checked to make sure all my words are spelled correctly.	
Total	

Unit 3 Project: 85 points possible

Rubric Point System:

5 points – This part of the project is outstanding.

4 points – This part of the project is very strong.

3 points – This part of the project shows a lot of effort.

2 points – This part of the project needs improvement.

1 point – This part of the project is missing.

Unit 5 Student Rubric

Rubric Point System:

5 points – This part of the project is outstanding.

4 points – This part of the project is very strong.

3 points – This part of the project shows a lot of effort.

2 points – This part of the project needs improvement.

1 point – This part of the project is missing.

In the appendix of the Student Text and Workbook, you will find Reviewer's Rubric 13.15, which readers can use to give the student feedback on the assignment.

Rubric for Unit 5 Project	
Because of Winn Dixie: The Musical Set Design	Points Earned
Setting Details • I have chosen four different settings from the story.	
• I have collected details from the story about the place.	
• I have collected details from the story about the time period.	
• I have collected details from the story about the climate and weather.	
Appropriate Pictures • My pictures accurately depict setting details from the story.	
• I have included pictures that show details about the place.	
• I have included pictures that show details about the time period.	
• I have included pictures that show details about the climate and weather.	
Responses to Questions • My written responses show how much I understand about how setting contributes to a story.	
• My written responses show what happens in each of my chosen settings.	

Unit 5 Student Rubric

Rubric for Unit 5 Project	
Because of Winn Dixie: The Musical Set Design	Points Earned
• My written responses show that I understand what stages of the plot occurred in each setting.	
• My written responses show my understanding of each setting's importance.	
Quality • I have created a complete project with the required number of elements.	
• I have created a high-quality project. I was careful, thoughtful, and creative.	
Effort • I worked hard on my project, and it reflects an appropriate amount of effort.	
Conventions • I have followed the rules for capitalization and punctuation.	
• I have checked to make sure all my words are spelled correctly.	
Total	

Unit 5 Project: 85 points possible

Rubric Point System:

5 points – This part of the project is outstanding.

4 points – This part of the project is very strong.

3 points – This part of the project shows a lot of effort.

2 points – This part of the project needs improvement.

1 point – This part of the project is missing.

Checklist for Module 1

Directions: When you have completed a task, make a ✔ in the "Done" column. Ask a parent, teacher, or reading coach to award you points for each task using the checklist point system. Fill in the points you have earned on the SLEUTH'S LOG in the appendix.

Checklist Point System:

1–6 points may be awarded by a parent, teacher, or reading coach for each task completed. Here are the recommended guidelines:

6 – exemplary in quality *and* effort

5 – exemplary in either quality *or* effort

4 – acceptable in quality *and* effort

3 – acceptable in either quality *or* effort

2 – needs improvement in quality *and* effort

1 – incomplete

Tasks	Done ✔	Points Earned
1.4 Nonfiction or Fiction • List examples of nonfiction and fiction books that you have in your home.		
1.5 Narrative or Nonnarrative • List examples of narrative and nonnarrative books that you have in your home.		
1.7 Why Genre Matters • Find a book in your home or library that fits each genre listed and fill in the chart with the book titles.		
• Examine the different parts of each book and talk about the differences you notice with a parent, teacher, or reading coach.		
1.8 Introduction to Historical Fiction • Discuss the unique features of a historical fiction book with a parent, teacher, or reading coach.		
1.9 The Cover of *Sarah, Plain and Tall* (*SPT*) • Answer the questions by using the clues you find on the front and back covers of the book.		
1.10 Clues to Genre • Write your best ideas for answers to these questions.		
• Discuss your answers to the questions with a parent, teacher, or reading coach.		

Tasks	Done ✓	Points Earned
1.11 Make a Prediction • Write your predictions about what you expect to happen based on the clues you find on the cover of *SPT.*		
• Discuss your answers to the questions with a parent, teacher, or reading coach.		
1.12 Create Your Own Book Cover • Create a front and back cover for a book you might like to write someday.		
• Include plenty of clues for your readers so they will know what they can expect to find inside.		
• Ask several family members and friends to use the questions in 1.9 and 1.11 to answer questions about your cover.		
1.13 Review: Reader's Questions • Discuss your answers to the Reader's Questions from the beginning of the module with a parent, teacher, or reading coach.		
1.14 Book Talk • Use the questions to get a discussion going about the books your family or friends enjoy.		
Total		

Module 1: 90 points possible

Checklist Point System:

1–6 points may be awarded by a parent, teacher, or reading coach for each task completed. Here are the recommended guidelines:

6 – exemplary in quality *and* effort

5 – exemplary in either quality *or* effort

4 – acceptable in quality *and* effort

3 – acceptable in either quality *or* effort

2 – needs improvement in quality *and* effort

1 – incomplete

Checklist for Module 2

Directions: When you have completed a task, make a ✔ in the "Done" column. Ask a parent, teacher, or reading coach to award you points for each task using the checklist point system. Fill in the points you have earned on the SLEUTH'S LOG in the appendix.

Checklist Point System:

1–6 points may be awarded by a parent, teacher, or reading coach for each task completed. Here are the recommended guidelines:

6 – exemplary in quality *and* effort

5 – exemplary in either quality *or* effort

4 – acceptable in quality *and* effort

3 – acceptable in either quality *or* effort

2 – needs improvement in quality *and* effort

1 – incomplete

Tasks	Done ✔	Points Earned
2.3 Main, Major, and Minor Characters • Write down a main, major, and minor character from three of your favorite books.		
2.5 Read *Sarah, Plain and Tall*: Chapter 1 • Read chapter 1 of *SPT*.		
• List the characters you meet on the chart.		
• Write some of the details you learn about each character.		
• List how you learned each detail about the characters.		
2.6 Ruminate: Chapter 1 • Ruminate on the questions about chapter 1.		
• Discuss, draw, or write your answers to the questions.		
2.7 Aha! Chapter 1 • Answer the questions on the lines provided.		
• Refer to the chapter as you answer them.		
2.8 Read *Sarah, Plain and Tall*: Chapter 2 • Read chapter 2 of *SPT*.		
• From studying Sarah's letters in this chapter, list what you learn about Sarah and what you expect Sarah to be like when she arrives.		

Tasks	Done ✔	Points Earned
2.9 Ruminate: Chapter 2 • Ruminate on the questions about chapter 2.		
• Discuss, draw, or write your answers to the questions.		
2.10 Aha! Chapter 2 • Answer the questions on the lines provided.		
• Refer to the chapter as you answer them.		
2.12 Word Sleuth: Chapters 1–2 • Use context clues to make an educated guess about the meaning of the underlined word in each sentence. Write it on the line provided.		
• Look up the word in the RIR dictionary and compare your educated guess with the definition. Write the dictionary definition on the line provided.		
2.13 Conventions: I Spy Capitalization • Write down some of the rules for capitalization that you already know.		
• Answer the questions about the capitalized words you find in the book.		
2.14 Review: Reader's Questions • Discuss your answers to the Reader's Questions from the beginning of this module with a parent, teacher, or reading coach.		
2.15 Book Talk • Use the questions to get a discussion going about the books your family or friends enjoy.		
2.16 Sowing Seeds • Discuss these ideas with a parent, teacher, or reading coach.		
Total		

Module 2: 132 points possible

Checklist Point System:

1–6 points may be awarded by a parent, teacher, or reading coach for each task completed. Here are the recommended guidelines:

6 – exemplary in quality *and* effort

5 – exemplary in either quality *or* effort

4 – acceptable in quality *and* effort

3 – acceptable in either quality *or* effort

2 – needs improvement in quality *and* effort

1 – incomplete

Checklist for Module 3

Directions: When you have completed a task, make a ✔ in the "Done" column. Ask a parent, teacher, or reading coach to award you points for each task using the checklist point system. Fill in the points you have earned on the SLEUTH'S LOG in the appendix.

Checklist Point System:

1–6 points may be awarded by a parent, teacher, or reading coach for each task completed. Here are the recommended guidelines:

6 – exemplary in quality *and* effort

5 – exemplary in either quality *or* effort

4 – acceptable in quality *and* effort

3 – acceptable in either quality *or* effort

2 – needs improvement in quality *and* effort

1 – incomplete

Tasks	Done ✔	Points Earned
3.1 Making Inferences: Prior Knowledge • Review chapters 1–2 of *SPT*. Then describe what you think each character on the chart might look like.		
• Write the details in the story that help you make an educated guess.		
• Write any prior knowledge that helps you make an educated guess.		
• As you read chapters 3–6, add to all the columns on the chart.		
• Draw a picture or find an image of your favorite character so far.		
3.2 Character Development: Physical Traits • Answer the questions about your physical traits.		
• Answer the questions about Anna.		
• Discuss your answers with a parent, teacher, or reading coach.		
3.4 Character Development: Character Traits • Follow the instructions in this section and then answer the questions.		
3.5 Read *Sarah, Plain and Tall*: Chapter 3 • Read chapter 3 of *SPT*.		
• Add additional physical traits you find to the chart in 3.1 MAKING INFERENCES: PRIOR KNOWLEDGE.		
• List each character's character traits.		

Tasks	Done ✓	Points Earned
• List the details from the book that make you think this.		
• List the prior knowledge that makes you think this.		
3.6 A Time Machine for Chapter 3 • Draw three different events from chapter 3 that show the characters in action.		
• Show all the details Patricia MacLachlan includes about each event.		
• Add additional details you imagine in your mind.		
• Share your pictures with a parent, teacher, or reading coach.		
3.7 Read *Sarah, Plain and Tall:* Chapter 4 • Read chapter 4 of *SPT*.		
• Add additional physical traits you find to the chart in 3.1 Making Inferences: Prior Knowledge.		
• List differences between Sarah's home in Maine and her new home.		
3.8 Ruminate: Chapters 3–4 • Ruminate on the questions about chapters 3–4.		
• Discuss, draw, or write your answers to the questions.		
3.9 Aha! Chapters 3–4 • Answer the questions on the lines provided.		
• Refer to the chapters as you answer them.		
3.10 Word Sleuth: Chapters 3–4 • Use context clues to make an educated guess about the meaning of the underlined word in each sentence. Write it on the line provided.		

Checklist Point System:

1–6 points may be awarded by a parent, teacher, or reading coach for each task completed. Here are the recommended guidelines:

6 – exemplary in quality *and* effort

5 – exemplary in either quality *or* effort

4 – acceptable in quality *and* effort

3 – acceptable in either quality *or* effort

2 – needs improvement in quality *and* effort

1 – incomplete

Checklist Point System:

1–6 points may be awarded by a parent, teacher, or reading coach for each task completed. Here are the recommended guidelines:

6 – exemplary in quality *and* effort

5 – exemplary in either quality *or* effort

4 – acceptable in quality *and* effort

3 – acceptable in either quality *or* effort

2 – needs improvement in quality *and* effort

1 – incomplete

Tasks	Done ✓	Points Earned
• Look up the word in the RIR dictionary and compare your educated guess with the definition. Write the dictionary definition on the line provided.		
3.11 Conventions: What Is a Sentence? • Circle the organized groups of words and underline the unorganized groups of words.		
• Answer the questions about sentences and discuss your answers with a parent, teacher, or reading coach.		
• Write down the subject, predicate, and main verb of each complete sentence.		
3.12 Character Development: Changes and Challenges • List the changes and challenges that each character faces.		
3.13 Character Development: Responses • Create a comic strip about a change or a challenge you have faced.		
• Share your comic strip with a parent, teacher or reading coach.		
3.15 Read *Sarah, Plain and Tall*: Chapters 5–6 • Read chapters 5–6 of *SPT*.		
• List the changes and challenges that the characters face.		
• Write how each character responds to change and challenges.		
• List the evidence that shows you this.		
3.16 Ruminate: Chapters 5–6 • Ruminate on the questions about chapters 5–6.		
• Discuss, draw, or write your answers to the questions.		

Tasks	Done ✔	Points Earned
3.17 Aha! Chapters 5–6 • Answer the questions on the lines provided.		
• Refer to the chapters as you answer them.		
3.18 Word Sleuth: Chapters 5–6 • Use context clues to make an educated guess about the meaning of the underlined word in each sentence. Write it on the line provided.		
• Look up the word in the RIR dictionary and compare your educated guess with the definition. Write the dictionary definition on the line provided.		
3.19 Conventions: What Is a Paragraph? • Answer the questions on the lines provided.		
3.20 Review: Reader's Questions • Discuss your answers to the READER'S QUESTIONS from the beginning of this module with a parent, teacher, or reading coach.		
3.21 Book Talk • Use the questions to get a discussion going about the books your family or friends enjoy.		
3.22 Sowing Seeds • Discuss these ideas with a parent, teacher, or reading coach.		
Total		

Module 3: 282 points possible

Checklist Point System:

1–6 points may be awarded by a parent, teacher, or reading coach for each task completed. Here are the recommended guidelines:

6 – exemplary in quality *and* effort

5 – exemplary in either quality *or* effort

4 – acceptable in quality *and* effort

3 – acceptable in either quality *or* effort

2 – needs improvement in quality *and* effort

1 – incomplete

Checklist for Module 4

Directions: When you have completed a task, make a ✔ in the "Done" column. Ask a parent, teacher, or reading coach to award you points for each task using the checklist point system. Fill in the points you have earned on the SLEUTH'S LOG in the appendix.

Tasks	Done ✔	Points Earned
4.1 Character Development: Differences • Reread pages 12–14 of chapter 2 of *SPT*.		
• Use the Venn diagram to show how Anna and Caleb are similar.		
• Use the Venn diagram to show how Anna and Caleb are different.		
4.2 Read *Sarah, Plain and Tall:* Chapter 7 • Read chapter 7 of *SPT*.		
4.3 Aha! Chapter 7 • Answer the questions on the lines provided.		
• Refer to the chapter as you answer them.		
4.4 Theme: Something to Think About • Write down the similarities between the changes and challenges facing Anna and Caleb and the changes and challenges that you have faced or are facing right now.		
• Answer the questions about the repeated statement in *SPT*.		
4.5 Read *Sarah, Plain and Tall*: Chapter 8 • Read chapter 8 of *SPT*.		
4.6 Ruminate: Chapters 7–8 • Ruminate on the questions about chapters 7–8.		
• Discuss, draw, or write your answers to the questions.		

Checklist Point System:

1–6 points may be awarded by a parent, teacher, or reading coach for each task completed. Here are the recommended guidelines:

6 – exemplary in quality *and* effort

5 – exemplary in either quality *or* effort

4 – acceptable in quality *and* effort

3 – acceptable in either quality *or* effort

2 – needs improvement in quality *and* effort

1 – incomplete

Tasks	Done ✔	Points Earned
4.7 Aha! Chapter 8 • Answer the questions on the lines provided.		
• Refer to the chapter as you answer them.		
4.8 Character Development: Changes • Use the chart to write some of the new things you notice about the characters.		
4.9 Read *Sarah, Plain and Tall*: Chapter 9 • Read chapter 9 of *SPT*.		
• Describe how each character responds to Sarah's trip into town.		
4.10 Ruminate: Chapter 9 • Ruminate on the questions about chapter 9.		
• Discuss, draw, or write your answers to the questions.		
4.11 Aha! Chapter 9 • Answer the questions on the lines provided.		
• Refer to the chapter as you answer them.		
4.12 Word Sleuth: Chapters 7–9 • Use context clues to make an educated guess about the meaning of the underlined word in each sentence. Write it on the line provided.		
• Look up the word in the RIR dictionary and compare your educated guess with the definition. Write the dictionary definition on the line provided.		
4.13 Conventions: What Is a Chapter? • Answer the questions with your best ideas.		
4.14 Who Is the Main Character? • Use the list to plan and write a paragraph about who you think the main character of this story is.		
• Include examples from the book to support your choice.		

Checklist Point System:

1–6 points may be awarded by a parent, teacher, or reading coach for each task completed. Here are the recommended guidelines:

6 – exemplary in quality *and* effort

5 – exemplary in either quality *or* effort

4 – acceptable in quality *and* effort

3 – acceptable in either quality *or* effort

2 – needs improvement in quality *and* effort

1 – incomplete

Checklist Point System:

1–6 points may be awarded by a parent, teacher, or reading coach for each task completed. Here are the recommended guidelines:

6 – exemplary in quality *and* effort

5 – exemplary in either quality *or* effort

4 – acceptable in quality *and* effort

3 – acceptable in either quality *or* effort

2 – needs improvement in quality *and* effort

1 – incomplete

Tasks	Done ✓	Points Earned
4.15 Genre: Why Is *Sarah, Plain and Tall* Historical Fiction? • Provide details in each category that show that *SPT* is historical fiction.		
4.16 Unit Project: Character Map • Create a character map.		
• Use the rubric to score your character map. Record your score in the Points Earned column on the right.		
4.17 Review: Reader's Questions • Discuss your answers to the Reader's Questions from the beginning of this module with a parent, teacher, or reading coach.		
4.18 Book Talk • Use the questions to get a discussion going about the books your family or friends enjoy.		
4.19 Sowing Seeds • Discuss these ideas with a parent, teacher, or reading coach.		
Total		

Module 4: 174 points possible, plus 65 points possible for unit project

Checklist for Module 5

Directions: When you have completed a task, make a ✔ in the "Done" column. Ask a parent, teacher, or reading coach to award you points for each task using the checklist point system. Fill in the points you have earned on the SLEUTH'S LOG in the appendix.

Tasks	Done ✔	Points Earned
5.1 On My Own: Historical Fiction • Write the title and author of the book you have selected to study.		
• Explain briefly why you have chosen this book.		
• Print and affix an image of the book's cover.		
5.2 Reader's Questions • Write at least five questions that you hope will be answered as you read the book you've selected.		
• Talk about your questions with a parent, teacher, or reading coach.		
5.3 The Cover of My Historical Fiction Book • Answer the questions about the front and back covers of the book you've selected.		
5.4 Make a Prediction • Use the clues you gathered from the cover to make some predictions about what you expect to happen in this book.		
5.5 Meet the Author • With the help of a parent, teacher, or reading coach, research your author on the Internet.		
• Fill out the graphic organizer.		
• Print an image of the author and affix it to the space provided.		

Checklist Point System:

1–6 points may be awarded by a parent, teacher, or reading coach for each task completed. Here are the recommended guidelines:

6 – exemplary in quality *and* effort

5 – exemplary in either quality *or* effort

4 – acceptable in quality *and* effort

3 – acceptable in either quality *or* effort

2 – needs improvement in quality *and* effort

1 – incomplete

Checklist Point System:

1–6 points may be awarded by a parent, teacher, or reading coach for each task completed. Here are the recommended guidelines:

6 – exemplary in quality *and* effort

5 – exemplary in either quality *or* effort

4 – acceptable in quality *and* effort

3 – acceptable in either quality *or* effort

2 – needs improvement in quality *and* effort

1 – incomplete

Tasks	Done ✔	Points Earned
5.6 Read Your OYO Historical Fiction Book • Preview the activities in the unit before you read.		
• With the help of a parent, teacher, or reading coach, decide how much of your book you should read each day.		
• Write the schedule on the lines provided.		
• Read your OYO historical fiction book.		
5.7 Word Sleuth: On Your Own • As you read your OYO book, fill the chart with new words to add to your vocabulary.		
• Make an educated guess about the meaning of each word and record it on the chart.		
• Look up each word in a dictionary and record its definition on the chart.		
5.8 Ruminate: On Your Own • Ruminate on the questions about *SPT* and the beginning of your book.		
• Discuss, draw, or write your answers to the questions.		
• Ruminate on the questions about *SPT* and the middle of your book.		
• Discuss, draw, or write your answers to the questions.		
• Ruminate on the questions about the ending of your book.		
• Discuss, draw, or write your answers to the questions.		
5.9 Meet the Characters • Review the opening chapters of your OYO book.		
• On the chart list the characters you meet in the opening chapters.		

Tasks	Done ✓	Points Earned
• Write what you learned about each one and how you learned it.		
• Discuss your chart with a parent, teacher, or reading coach.		
5.10 Character Development: Physical Traits • Draw a picture of two characters from your OYO book.		
• List the details from your book that show the physical traits you depicted.		
• List any prior knowledge that helps you picture each character.		
5.11 Character Development: Character Traits • Review the middle chapters of your book.		
• List the character traits of a few major characters on the Character Traits chart.		
• List the details from your book that show the character traits you selected.		
• List any prior knowledge that helps you make these inferences.		
5.12 Character Development: Changes and Challenges • List the changes and challenges that each character faces.		
• Identify the main conflict that each character faces.		
• Explain your answers to a parent, teacher, or reading coach.		
5.13 Character Development: Responses • Review the remaining chapters of your historical fiction book. Pay attention to how the major characters respond to the challenges they face in the story.		

Checklist Point System:

1–6 points may be awarded by a parent, teacher, or reading coach for each task completed. Here are the recommended guidelines:

6 – exemplary in quality *and* effort

5 – exemplary in either quality *or* effort

4 – acceptable in quality *and* effort

3 – acceptable in either quality *or* effort

2 – needs improvement in quality *and* effort

1 – incomplete

Checklist Point System:

1–6 points may be awarded by a parent, teacher, or reading coach for each task completed. Here are the recommended guidelines:

6 – exemplary in quality *and* effort

5 – exemplary in either quality *or* effort

4 – acceptable in quality *and* effort

3 – acceptable in either quality *or* effort

2 – needs improvement in quality *and* effort

1 – incomplete

Tasks	Done ✔	Points Earned
• Choose two major characters in your book and note their responses to changes and challenges on the chart.		
• List details from the story that show these responses.		
5.14 Character Development: Differences • Choose a change or challenge in the book you've read and sketch the different ways two major characters respond to the same event.		
• Discuss your drawings with a parent, teacher, or reading coach.		
5.15 Character Development: Changes • List two major characters you meet in the story who learn something new, speak differently, act differently, or think differently because of events in the story.		
• Explain how each character has matured, grown, or changed.		
• Give details from the book to support your answers.		
5.16 Who Is the Main Character? • Use the graphic organizer to show who you think the main character is.		
• Give details from the story to support your answer.		
5.17 Character Development: Compare and Contrast • Decide which character in your historical fiction book is most like one of the characters in *SPT*.		
• Using the five areas of character development, list some of the ways the characters you have matched are similar.		
• Using the five areas of character development, list some of the ways the same characters you have matched are different.		

Tasks	Done ✓	Points Earned
5.18 Genre: Why Is Your Book Historical Fiction? • Provide details in each category that show why your book is historical fiction.		
5.19 Review: Reader's Questions • Discuss your answers to the READER'S QUESTIONS you created at the beginning of this module with a parent, teacher, or reading coach.		
5.20 Book Talk • Use the questions to get a discussion going about the books your family or friends enjoy.		
5.21 Sowing Seeds • Talk about these ideas with a parent, teacher, or reading coach.		
Total		

Module 5: 324 points possible

Checklist Point System:

1–6 points may be awarded by a parent, teacher, or reading coach for each task completed. Here are the recommended guidelines:

6 – exemplary in quality *and* effort

5 – exemplary in either quality *or* effort

4 – acceptable in quality *and* effort

3 – acceptable in either quality *or* effort

2 – needs improvement in quality *and* effort

1 – incomplete

Checklist for Module 6

Directions: When you have completed a task, make a ✔ in the "Done" column. Ask a parent, teacher, or reading coach to award you points for each task using the checklist point system. Fill in the points you have earned on the SLEUTH'S LOG in the appendix.

Checklist Point System:

1–6 points may be awarded by a parent, teacher, or reading coach for each task completed. Here are the recommended guidelines:

6 – exemplary in quality *and* effort

5 – exemplary in either quality *or* effort

4 – acceptable in quality *and* effort

3 – acceptable in either quality *or* effort

2 – needs improvement in quality *and* effort

1 – incomplete

Tasks	Done ✔	Points Earned
6.1 Introduction to Animal Fantasy • Discuss the unique features of an animal fantasy book with a parent, teacher, or reading coach.		
6.2 The Parts of *Charlotte's Web* • Answer the questions based on your examination of the book.		
6.3 Make a Prediction • Answer the questions based on the information you collect from the table of contents.		
6.4 Read Kate DiCamillo's Foreword • Read the foreword by Kate DiCamillo.		
• Answer the questions on the lines provided.		
6.8 Read *Charlotte's Web*: Chapters I–III • Read chapters I–III of *CW*.		
• Fill in the CHARACTER INTRODUCTIONS chart with details about the characters.		
• Fill in the SETTING chart with details that show the time period and the place of the story.		
6.9 Ruminate: Chapters I–III • Ruminate on the questions about chapters I–III.		
• Discuss, draw, or write your answers to the questions.		
6.10 Aha! Chapters I–III • Answer the questions on the lines provided.		

Tasks	Done ✓	Points Earned
• Refer to the chapters as you answer them.		
6.11 Reading Strategies: Denotations and Connotations of Words • Think of the images and experiences that you picture when you read the underlined word and write them on the line provided.		
• Identify the emotions you associate with the underlined word and write them on the line provided.		
• Indicate whether the connotations of the word are positive, negative, or neutral.		
6.12 Word Sleuth: Chapters I–III • Use context clues to make an educated guess about the meaning of the underlined word in each sentence. Write it on the line provided.		
• Look up the word in the RIR dictionary and compare your educated guess with the definition. Write the dictionary definition on the line provided.		
6.13 Conventions: I Spy Italics • Find the italicized words on the chart in the foreword or chapter I.		
• Make an inference about why these words are italicized.		
6.14 Read *Charlotte's Web*: Chapters IV–VII • Read chapters IV–VII of *CW*.		
• Fill in the Animal and Human Behaviors chart with examples of animal behavior and human behavior for each character listed.		
6.15 Ruminate: Chapters IV–VII • Ruminate on the questions about chapters IV–VII.		
• Discuss, draw, or write your answers to the questions.		
6.16 Aha! Chapters IV–VII • Answer the questions on the lines provided.		
• Refer to the chapters as you answer them.		

Checklist Point System:

1–6 points may be awarded by a parent, teacher, or reading coach for each task completed. Here are the recommended guidelines:

6 – exemplary in quality *and* effort

5 – exemplary in either quality *or* effort

4 – acceptable in quality *and* effort

3 – acceptable in either quality *or* effort

2 – needs improvement in quality *and* effort

1 – incomplete

Checklist Point System:

1–6 points may be awarded by a parent, teacher, or reading coach for each task completed. Here are the recommended guidelines:

6 – exemplary in quality *and* effort

5 – exemplary in either quality *or* effort

4 – acceptable in quality *and* effort

3 – acceptable in either quality *or* effort

2 – needs improvement in quality *and* effort

1 – incomplete

Tasks	Done ✔	Points Earned
6.17 Plot: Inciting Incident • Determine the inciting incident in *Sarah, Plain and Tall.*		
• Write your answer with a brief explanation.		
6.18 Word Work: Connotations • Read the sentence and discuss the words that describe Wilbur with a parent, teacher, or reading coach.		
• Identify the emotion you associate with each underlined word.		
• Indicate whether the connotations of the word are positive, negative, or neutral.		
6.19 Word Sleuth: Chapters IV–VII • Use context clues to make an educated guess about the meaning of the underlined word in each sentence. Write it on the line provided.		
• Look up the word in the RIR dictionary and compare your educated guess with the definition. Write the dictionary definition on the line provided.		
6.20 Review: Reader's Questions • Discuss your answers to the Reader's Questions from the beginning of this module with a parent, teacher, or reading coach.		
6.21 Book Talk • Use the questions to get a discussion going about the books your family or friends enjoy.		
6.22 Sowing Seeds • Discuss these ideas with a parent, teacher, or reading coach.		
Total		

Module 6: 210 points possible

Checklist for Module 7

Directions: When you have completed a task, make a ✔ in the "Done" column. Ask a parent, teacher, or reading coach to award you points for each task using the checklist point system. Fill in the points you have earned on the SLEUTH'S LOG in the appendix.

Tasks	Done ✔	Points Earned
7.1 Character Development: Who Wants What? • Answer the questions on the lines provided.		
• For each character listed on the chart, identify at least one thing each character wants. Review the first seven chapters of *CW* to help you.		
• For each character listed on the chart, identify at least one obstacle in the character's way. Review the first seven chapters of *CW* to help you.		
7.3 Read *Charlotte's Web*: Chapters VIII–X • Read chapters VIII–X of *CW*. Notice when the events cause you to feel stress or concern for the characters.		
• Complete the CONFLICT COMPLICATIONS chart.		
7.4 Ruminate: Chapters VIII–X • Ruminate on the questions about chapters VIII–X.		
• Discuss, draw, or write your answers to the questions.		
7.5 Aha! Chapters VIII–X • Answer the questions on the lines provided.		
• Refer to the chapters as you answer them.		
7.6 Word Work: I Spy a Synonym • Answer the questions about the sentence from page 46 of *CW*.		

Checklist Point System:

1–6 points may be awarded by a parent, teacher, or reading coach for each task completed. Here are the recommended guidelines:

6 – exemplary in quality *and* effort

5 – exemplary in either quality *or* effort

4 – acceptable in quality *and* effort

3 – acceptable in either quality *or* effort

2 – needs improvement in quality *and* effort

1 – incomplete

Checklist Point System:

1–6 points may be awarded by a parent, teacher, or reading coach for each task completed. Here are the recommended guidelines:

6 – exemplary in quality *and* effort

5 – exemplary in either quality *or* effort

4 – acceptable in quality *and* effort

3 – acceptable in either quality *or* effort

2 – needs improvement in quality *and* effort

1 – incomplete

Tasks	Done ✓	Points Earned
7.7 Word Sleuth: Chapters VIII–X • Use context clues to make an educated guess about the meaning of the underlined word in each sentence. Write it on the line provided.		
• Look up the word in the RIR dictionary and compare your educated guess with the definition. Write the dictionary definition on the line provided.		
7.8 Figures of Speech: I Spy Onomatopoeia • Create onomatopoetic words for the sounds provided.		
7.9 Read *Charlotte's Web*: Chapters XI–XII • Read chapters XI–XII of *CW*. Look for how the main problem becomes more complicated in this section.		
7.10 Ruminate: Chapters XI–XII • Ruminate on the questions about chapters XI–XII.		
• Discuss, draw, or write your answers to the questions.		
7.11 Aha! Chapters XI–XII • Answer the questions on the lines provided.		
• Refer to the chapters as you answer them.		
7.12 Word Sleuth: Chapters XI–XII • Make an educated guess about the meaning of the underlined word in each sentence. Write it on the line provided.		
• Look up the word in the RIR dictionary and compare your educated guess with the definition. Write the dictionary definition on the line provided.		
7.13 Conventions: I Spy Punctuation • Identify the punctuation marks on the PUNCTUATION chart.		
• List the page number where each punctuation mark occurs.		

Tasks	Done ✔	Points Earned
• List the rule you think White is following when he uses each mark.		
7.14 Plot: Reveals Character • Fill in the missing information on the chart.		
7.15 Review: Reader's Questions • Discuss your answers to the Reader's Questions from the beginning of this module with a parent, teacher, or reading coach.		
7.16 Book Talk • Use the questions to get a discussion going about the books your family or friends enjoy.		
7.17 Sowing Seeds • Discuss these ideas with a parent, teacher, or reading coach.		
Total		

Module 7: 162 points possible

Checklist Point System:

1–6 points may be awarded by a parent, teacher, or reading coach for each task completed. Here are the recommended guidelines:

6 – exemplary in quality *and* effort

5 – exemplary in either quality *or* effort

4 – acceptable in quality *and* effort

3 – acceptable in either quality *or* effort

2 – needs improvement in quality *and* effort

1 – incomplete

Checklist for Module 8

Directions: When you have completed a task, make a ✔ in the "Done" column. Ask a parent, teacher, or reading coach to award you points for each task using the checklist point system. Fill in the points you have earned on the SLEUTH'S LOG in the appendix.

Checklist Point System:

1–6 points may be awarded by a parent, teacher, or reading coach for each task completed. Here are the recommended guidelines:

6 – exemplary in quality *and* effort

5 – exemplary in either quality *or* effort

4 – acceptable in quality *and* effort

3 – acceptable in either quality *or* effort

2 – needs improvement in quality *and* effort

1 – incomplete

Tasks	Done ✔	Points Earned
8.2 Read *Charlotte's Web*: Chapters XIII–XIV • Read chapters XIII–XIV of *CW*. As you read, think about how E. B. White makes you care more deeply about the characters in the story.		
• Fill in the REASONS I CARE chart with your answers.		
8.3 Ruminate: Chapters XIII–XIV • Ruminate on the questions about chapters XIII–XIV.		
• Discuss, draw, or write your answers to the questions.		
8.4 Aha! Chapters XIII–XIV • Answer the questions on the lines provided.		
• Refer to the chapters as you answer them.		
8.5 Reading Strategies: More Clues in Context • Answer the questions about the spider's web.		
8.6 Word Sleuth: Chapters XIII–XIV • Make an educated guess about the meaning of the underlined word in each sentence. Write it on the line provided.		
• Look up the word in the RIR dictionary and compare your educated guess with the definition. Write the dictionary definition on the line provided.		
8.7 Conventions: I Spy a Simple Sentence • Write the possible reasons we use different types of punctuation marks in sentences on the lines provided.		

Tasks	Done ✔	Points Earned
• List the five sentences on page 93 of *CW* that contain only a period and no other punctuation marks.		
• List the subject and the main verb of each sentence from page 93.		
8.9 Read *Charlotte's Web*: Chapters XV–XVI • Read chapters XV–XVI of *CW*. Notice how E. B. White keeps the action rising throughout this section.		
8.10 Ruminate: Chapters XV–XVI • Ruminate on the questions about chapters XV–XVI.		
• Discuss, draw, or write your answers to the questions.		
8.11 Aha! Chapters XV–XVI • Answer the questions on the lines provided.		
• Refer to the chapters as you answer them.		
8.12 Word Sleuth: Chapters XV–XVI • Make an educated guess about the meaning of the underlined word in each sentence. Write it on the line provided.		
• Look up the word in the RIR dictionary and compare your educated guess with the definition. Write the dictionary definition on the line provided.		
8.13 Review: Reader's Questions • Discuss your answers to the Reader's Questions from the beginning of this module with a parent, teacher, or reading coach.		
8.14 Book Talk • Use the questions to get a discussion going about the books your family or friends enjoy.		
8.15 Sowing Seeds • Discuss these ideas with a parent, teacher, or reading coach.		
Total		

Module 8: 132 points possible

Checklist Point System:

1–6 points may be awarded by a parent, teacher, or reading coach for each task completed. Here are the recommended guidelines:

6 – exemplary in quality *and* effort

5 – exemplary in either quality *or* effort

4 – acceptable in quality *and* effort

3 – acceptable in either quality *or* effort

2 – needs improvement in quality *and* effort

1 – incomplete

Checklist for Module 9

Directions: When you have completed a task, make a ✔ in the "Done" column. Ask a parent, teacher, or reading coach to award you points for each task using the checklist point system. Fill in the points you have earned on the SLEUTH'S LOG in the appendix.

Checklist Point System:

1–6 points may be awarded by a parent, teacher, or reading coach for each task completed. Here are the recommended guidelines:

6 – exemplary in quality *and* effort

5 – exemplary in either quality *or* effort

4 – acceptable in quality *and* effort

3 – acceptable in either quality *or* effort

2 – needs improvement in quality *and* effort

1 – incomplete

Tasks	Done ✔	Points Earned
9.1 Look How Far You've Come • On the chart, write one or two sentences about what has happened in each stage of the plot so far.		
9.2 Plot: Recognizing the Climax • Reread chapter 9 of *Sarah, Plain and Tall* from the beginning to the middle of page 64.		
• Discuss the questions listed with a parent, teacher, or reading coach.		
• Discuss how Patricia MacLachlan uses one of the options listed to create the climax with a parent, teacher or reading coach.		
9.3. Plot: Falling Action and Resolution • Reread the last chapter of *SPT* from page 64 to the end of the book.		
• Discuss the questions about the falling action and resolution in *SPT* with a parent, teacher, or reading coach.		
9.4 Make a Prediction • On the lines provided, predict which of these chapters will be part of the rising action, climax, falling action, and resolution of this story.		
• State the clues in the titles that help you to make your predictions.		
9.5 Read *Charlotte's Web*: Chapters XVII–XIX • Predict what you think E. B. White might do in these chapters to keep readers reading.		

Tasks	Done ✔	Points Earned
• Read chapters XVII–XIX of *CW*.		
9.6 Ruminate: Chapters XVII–XIX • Ruminate on the questions about chapters XVII–XIX.		
• Discuss, draw, or write your answers to the questions.		
9.7 Aha! Chapters XVII–XIX • Answer the questions on the lines provided.		
• Refer to the chapters as you answer them.		
9.8 Word Sleuth: Chapters XVII–XIX • Make an educated guess about the meaning of the underlined word in each sentence. Write it on the line provided.		
• Look up the word in the RIR dictionary and compare your educated guess with the definition. Write the dictionary definition on the line provided.		
9.9 Read *Charlotte's Web*: Chapters XX–XXII • Read chapters XX–XXII of *CW*.		
• Use the chart to list the events that occur in each stage of the plot.		
9.10 Ruminate: Chapters XX–XXII • Ruminate on the questions about chapters XX–XXII.		
• Discuss, draw, or write your answers to the questions.		
9.11 Aha! Chapters XX–XXII • Answer the questions on the lines provided.		
• Refer to the chapters as you answer them.		
9.12 Word Sleuth: Chapters XX–XXII • Make an educated guess about the meaning of the underlined word in each sentence. Write it on the line provided.		

Checklist Point System:

1–6 points may be awarded by a parent, teacher, or reading coach for each task completed. Here are the recommended guidelines:

6 – exemplary in quality *and* effort

5 – exemplary in either quality *or* effort

4 – acceptable in quality *and* effort

3 – acceptable in either quality *or* effort

2 – needs improvement in quality *and* effort

1 – incomplete

Checklist Point System:

1–6 points may be awarded by a parent, teacher, or reading coach for each task completed. Here are the recommended guidelines:

6 – exemplary in quality *and* effort

5 – exemplary in either quality *or* effort

4 – acceptable in quality *and* effort

3 – acceptable in either quality *or* effort

2 – needs improvement in quality *and* effort

1 – incomplete

Tasks	Done ✓	Points Earned
• Look up the word in the RIR dictionary and compare your educated guess with the definition. Write the dictionary definition on the line provided.		
9.13 Recognizing the Climax of *Charlotte's Web* • Sketch or describe one event from each plot stage in *Charlotte's Web.*		
9.14 Genre: Why Is *Charlotte's Web* an Animal Fantasy? • Provide details in each category that show *CW* is an animal fantasy.		
9.15 Unit Project: Storyboard • Create a storyboard of the plot for a story you invent.		
• Draw an illustration for an event in each stage of the plot.		
• Use the rubric to score your storyboard. Record your score in the Points Earned column on the right.		
9.16 Review: Reader's Questions • Discuss your answers to the READER'S QUESTIONS from the beginning of this module with a parent, teacher, or reading coach.		
9.17 Book Talk • Use the questions to get a discussion going about the books your family or friends enjoy.		
9.18 Sowing Seeds • Discuss these ideas with a parent, teacher, or reading coach.		
Total		

Module 9: 174 points possible, plus 85 points possible for unit project.

Checklist for Module 10

Directions: When you have completed a task, make a ✔ in the "Done" column. Ask a parent, teacher, or reading coach to award you points for each task using the checklist point system. Fill in the points you have earned on the SLEUTH'S LOG in the appendix.

Tasks	Done ✔	Points Earned
10.1 On My Own: Animal Fantasy • Write the title and author of the book you have selected to study.		
• Explain briefly why this book captured your attention.		
• Print an image of the book's cover and affix it to the space provided.		
10.2 Reader's Questions • Write at least five questions that you hope will be answered as you read the book you've selected.		
• Talk about your questions with a parent, teacher, or reading coach.		
10.3 The Cover of My Animal Fantasy Book • Answer the questions about the front and back covers of the book you've selected.		
10.4 Make a Prediction • Use the clues you gathered from the cover and other parts of the book to make some predictions about what you expect to happen in this book.		
10.5 Meet the Author • With the help of a parent, teacher, or reading coach, research your author on the Internet.		
• Fill in the graphic organizer.		
• Print an image of the author and affix it to the space provided.		

Checklist Point System:

1–6 points may be awarded by a parent, teacher, or reading coach for each task completed. Here are the recommended guidelines:

6 – exemplary in quality *and* effort

5 – exemplary in either quality *or* effort

4 – acceptable in quality *and* effort

3 – acceptable in either quality *or* effort

2 – needs improvement in quality *and* effort

1 – incomplete

Checklist Point System:

1–6 points may be awarded by a parent, teacher, or reading coach for each task completed. Here are the recommended guidelines:

6 – exemplary in quality *and* effort

5 – exemplary in either quality *or* effort

4 – acceptable in quality *and* effort

3 – acceptable in either quality *or* effort

2 – needs improvement in quality *and* effort

1 – incomplete

Tasks	Done ✓	Points Earned
10.6 Read Your OYO Animal Fantasy • Preview the activities in the unit before you read.		
• With the help of a parent, teacher, or reading coach, decide how much of your book you should read each day.		
• Write the schedule on the lines provided.		
• Read your OYO animal fantasy.		
10.7 Word Sleuth: On Your Own • As you read your OYO book, fill the chart with new words to add to your vocabulary.		
• Make an educated guess about the meaning of each word and record it on the chart.		
• Look up each word in the dictionary and record its definition on the chart.		
10.8 Ruminate: On Your Own • Ruminate on the questions about the beginning of your book.		
• Discuss, draw, or write your answers to the questions.		
• Ruminate on the questions about the middle of your book.		
• Discuss, draw, or write your answers to the questions.		
• Ruminate on the ending of your book.		
• Discuss, draw, or write your answers to the questions.		
10.9 Plot: Exposition • Complete the chart with details about the time and place of the setting.		
• Complete the chart with details about the characters.		
10.10 Character Development: Who Wants What? • List the major characters the author introduces in the first several chapters of your book.		

Tasks	Done ✓	Points Earned
• Identify at least one thing each character wants.		
• Identify at least one thing that gets in the way of each character's desire.		
10.11 Plot: Inciting Incident • Identify the inciting incident in your book.		
• Explain your answer.		
• Discuss your answer with a parent, teacher, or reading coach.		
10.12 Plot: Rising Action • List two of the major characters in your book and each character's problem.		
• Explain how the problem gets more complicated. Use details from the book to support your choice.		
• Discuss your answer with a parent, teacher, or reading coach.		
10.13 Plot: The Climax • Answer the questions about the climax of your book.		
• Include details from the book to support your answers.		
• Discuss your answers with a parent, teacher, or reading coach.		
10.14 Plot: Falling Action and Resolution • Answer the questions about the falling action and resolution of your book.		
• Include details from the book to support your answers.		
• Discuss your answers with a parent, teacher, or reading coach.		
10.15 Plot Development: Compare and Contrast • Describe what happens in each plot event in each book.		
• List any similarities and differences you notice.		
• Discuss your answers with a parent, teacher, or reading coach.		

Checklist Point System:

1–6 points may be awarded by a parent, teacher, or reading coach for each task completed. Here are the recommended guidelines:

6 – exemplary in quality *and* effort

5 – exemplary in either quality *or* effort

4 – acceptable in quality *and* effort

3 – acceptable in either quality *or* effort

2 – needs improvement in quality *and* effort

1 – incomplete

Checklist Point System:

1–6 points may be awarded by a parent, teacher, or reading coach for each task completed. Here are the recommended guidelines:

6 – exemplary in quality *and* effort

5 – exemplary in either quality *or* effort

4 – acceptable in quality *and* effort

3 – acceptable in either quality *or* effort

2 – needs improvement in quality *and* effort

1 – incomplete

Tasks	Done ✓	Points Earned
10.16 Genre: Why Is Your Book Animal Fantasy? • Provide details in each category to show that your book is an animal fantasy.		
10.17 Review: Reader's Questions • Discuss your answers to the Reader's Questions you created at the beginning of this module with a parent, teacher, or reading coach.		
10.18 Book Talk • Use the questions to get a discussion going about the books your family or friends enjoy.		
10.19 Sowing Seeds • Discuss these ideas with a parent, teacher, or reading coach.		
Total		

Module 10: 282 points possible

Checklist for Module 11

Directions: When you have completed a task, make a ✔ in the "Done" column. Ask a parent, teacher, or reading coach to award you points for each task using the checklist point system. Fill in the points you have earned on the SLEUTH'S LOG in the appendix.

Tasks	Done ✔	Points Earned
11.1 The Cover of *Because of Winn-Dixie* • Answer the questions by using the clues you find on the front and back covers of this book.		
11.2 Introduction to Contemporary Realistic Fiction • Discuss the unique features of contemporary realistic fiction with a parent, teacher, or reading coach.		
11.3 Setting: Where and When • Complete the MY LIFE: HERE AND NOW chart.		
• Take a photograph of yourself somewhere that shows as much as possible about the setting for your life.		
11.4 Setting: It's in the Details • Complete the chart with clues you might include in a story about your life.		
• Ask a sibling or friend to guess where and when your story takes place.		
11.5 Setting: *Sarah, Plain and Tall* • With the help of a parent, teacher, or reading coach, research another time period.		
• List five things that would change in your life if you lived during this time period.		
11.6 Setting: *Charlotte's Web* • Answer the questions about the setting of *Charlotte's Web.* Refer back to the book.		
11.7 Read *Because of Winn-Dixie*: Chapters 1–5 • Read chapters 1–5 of *BWD.*		

Checklist Point System:

1–6 points may be awarded by a parent, teacher, or reading coach for each task completed. Here are the recommended guidelines:

6 – exemplary in quality *and* effort

5 – exemplary in either quality *or* effort

4 – acceptable in quality *and* effort

3 – acceptable in either quality *or* effort

2 – needs improvement in quality *and* effort

1 – incomplete

Tasks	Done ✔	Points Earned
• Complete the chart by comparing and contrasting the opening of *BWD* with one of the other books you have read this year.		
• Explain your answers to a parent, teacher, or reading coach.		
11.8 Ruminate: Chapters 1–5 • Ruminate on the questions about chapters 1–5.		
• Discuss, draw, or write your answers to the questions.		
11.9 Aha! Chapters 1–5 • Answer the questions on the lines provided.		
• Refer to the chapters as you answer them.		
11.10 The Plot of *Because of Winn-Dixie* • Answer the questions about the plot so far.		
11.11 Setting: *Because of Winn-Dixie* • List some of the details about where and when the events occur in the story so far.		
• Use the chart in 11.3 SETTING: WHERE AND WHEN to help you.		
11.12 Figures of Speech: I Spy Metaphors and Similes • Fill in the blank to create your own metaphor.		
• Answer the questions about the metaphors and similes in the sentences from *BWD*.		
11.14 Setting Affects the Plot • Write down three things the setting allows Opal to do.		
• Write down three things the setting prevents Opal from doing.		
11.15 Read *Because of Winn-Dixie*: Chapters 6–10 • Read chapters 6–10 of *BWD*.		

Checklist Point System:

1–6 points may be awarded by a parent, teacher, or reading coach for each task completed. Here are the recommended guidelines:

6 – exemplary in quality *and* effort

5 – exemplary in either quality *or* effort

4 – acceptable in quality *and* effort

3 – acceptable in either quality *or* effort

2 – needs improvement in quality *and* effort

1 – incomplete

Tasks	Done ✔	Points Earned
• Fill out the chart with information about three characters you meet in chapters 6–10.		
11.16 Ruminate: Chapters 6–10 • Ruminate on the questions about chapters 6–10.		
• Discuss, draw, or write your answers to the questions.		
11.17 Aha! Chapters 6–10 • Answer the questions on the lines provided.		
• Refer to the chapters as you answer them.		
11.18 Figures of Speech: Hyperbole • Explain the point that the hyperbole emphasizes in each sentence.		
11.19 Review: Reader's Questions • Discuss your answers to the READER'S QUESTIONS from the beginning of this module with a parent, teacher, or reading coach.		
11.20 Book Talk • Use the suggestions to get a discussion going about the books your family or friends enjoy.		
11.21 Sowing Seeds • Talk about these ideas with a parent, teacher, or reading coach.		
Total		

Module 11: 198 points possible

Checklist Point System:

1–6 points may be awarded by a parent, teacher, or reading coach for each task completed. Here are the recommended guidelines:

6 – exemplary in quality *and* effort

5 – exemplary in either quality *or* effort

4 – acceptable in quality *and* effort

3 – acceptable in either quality *or* effort

2 – needs improvement in quality *and* effort

1 – incomplete

Checklist for Module 12

Directions: When you have completed a task, make a ✔ in the "Done" column. Ask a parent, teacher, or reading coach to award you points for each task using the checklist point system. Fill in the points you have earned on the SLEUTH'S LOG in the appendix.

Checklist Point System:

1–6 points may be awarded by a parent, teacher, or reading coach for each task completed. Here are the recommended guidelines:

6 – exemplary in quality *and* effort

5 – exemplary in either quality *or* effort

4 – acceptable in quality *and* effort

3 – acceptable in either quality *or* effort

2 – needs improvement in quality *and* effort

1 – incomplete

Tasks	Done ✔	Points Earned
12.1 Setting Reveals Character: Part 1 • List three inferences you can make about snow leopards based on their habitat.		
• List three inferences someone could make about you just from your bedroom.		
• Identify the location where you meet each character listed on the chart.		
• List inferences you can draw about each character from studying his or her surroundings.		
12.2 Read *Because of Winn-Dixie*: Chapters 11–14 • Read chapters 11–14 of *BWD*.		
• List new things you learn about each character Opal interacts with.		
12.3 Ruminate: Chapters 11–14 • Ruminate on the questions about chapters 11–14.		
• Discuss, draw, or write your answers to the questions.		
12.4 Aha! Chapter 11–14 • Answer the questions on the lines provided.		
• Refer to the chapters as you answer them.		
12.5 Setting Reveals Character: Part 2 • List similarities and differences between lions and snow leopards.		
• Choose two different settings from *BWD* and answer the questions about them on the Venn diagram.		

Tasks	Done ✓	Points Earned
12.6 Plot: Episodic Structure • Reread chapters 5 and 11.		
• List the inciting incident, rising action, climax, and falling action in each chapter.		
12.7 Figures of Speech: I Spy Similes		
• Write five similes that you might hear at your house.		
• Underline the simile in each sentence.		
• Circle the word or words that signal the beginning of a simile.		
• Rewrite each sentence with a new simile.		
12.8 Read *Because of Winn-Dixie*: Chapters 15–19 • Read chapters 15–19 of *BWD*.		
• List what the Littmus Lozenge reminds each character of.		
• Make an inference about each character based on his or her reaction.		
12.9 Ruminate: Chapters 15–19 • Ruminate on the questions about chapters 15–19.		
• Discuss, draw, or write your answers to the questions.		
12.10 Aha! Chapters 15–19 • Answer the questions on the lines provided.		
• Refer to the chapters as you answer them.		
12.11 Review: Reader's Questions • Discuss your answers to the Reader's Questions from the beginning of this module with a parent, teacher, or reading coach.		
12.12 Book Talk • Use the questions to get a discussion going about the books your family or friends enjoy.		
12.13 Sowing Seeds • Talk about these ideas with a parent, teacher, or reading coach.		
Total		

Module 12: 174 points possible

Checklist Point System:

1–6 points may be awarded by a parent, teacher, or reading coach for each task completed. Here are the recommended guidelines:

6 – exemplary in quality *and* effort

5 – exemplary in either quality *or* effort

4 – acceptable in quality *and* effort

3 – acceptable in either quality *or* effort

2 – needs improvement in quality *and* effort

1 – incomplete

Checklist for Module 13

Directions: When you have completed a task, make a ✔ in the "Done" column. Ask a parent, teacher, or reading coach to award you points for each task using the checklist point system. Fill in the points you have earned on the SLEUTH'S LOG in the appendix.

Checklist Point System:

1–6 points may be awarded by a parent, teacher, or reading coach for each task completed. Here are the recommended guidelines:

6 – exemplary in quality *and* effort

5 – exemplary in either quality *or* effort

4 – acceptable in quality *and* effort

3 – acceptable in either quality *or* effort

2 – needs improvement in quality *and* effort

1 – incomplete

Tasks	Done ✔	Points Earned
13.1 The Story So Far • Answer the questions about *BWD* using details from the book.		
• Discuss your answers with a parent, teacher, or reading coach.		
13.2 Make a Prediction • Write your answers to the questions about foreshadowing.		
• Discuss your predictions about the outcome of *BWD* with a parent, teacher, or reading coach.		
13.3 Read *Because of Winn-Dixie*: Chapters 20–22 • Read chapters 20–22 of *BWD*.		
• List the events in this section that add anticipation or tension to the story.		
13.4 Ruminate: Chapters 20–22 • Ruminate on the questions about chapters 20–22.		
• Discuss, draw, or write your answers to the questions about these chapters of your book.		
13.5 Aha! Chapters 20–22 • Answer the questions on the lines provided.		
• Refer to the chapters as you answer them.		

Tasks	Done ✔	Points Earned
13.6 Figures of Speech: Personification • Answer the questions with your best ideas on the lines provided and discuss your answers with a parent, teacher, or reading coach.		
13.7 Character Development: Is Winn-Dixie a Character? • Explain in complete sentences what makes someone a character in a story.		
• Give your best reasons why you believe Winn-Dixie is or is not a character in the story. Use complete sentences.		
• Use details from the book to support your reasons.		
13.9 Read *Because of Winn-Dixie*: Chapters 23–26 • Read chapters 23–26 of *BWD*.		
• Fill out the chart with your best ideas.		
13.10 Ruminate: Chapters 23–26 • Ruminate on the questions about chapters 23–26.		
• Discuss, draw, or write your answers to the questions.		
13.11 Aha! Chapters 23–26 • Answer the questions on the lines provided.		
• Refer to the chapters as you answer them.		
13.12 Theme: Something to Think About • Find the statement in the final chapters repeated by two characters and write it on the lines provided.		
• Discuss what you think it means with a parent, teacher, or reading coach.		
13.13 Genre: Why Is *Because of Winn-Dixie* Contemporary Realistic Fiction? • Provide details in each category to show that *BWD* is contemporary realistic fiction.		

Checklist Point System:

1–6 points may be awarded by a parent, teacher, or reading coach for each task completed. Here are the recommended guidelines:

6 – exemplary in quality *and* effort

5 – exemplary in either quality *or* effort

4 – acceptable in quality *and* effort

3 – acceptable in either quality *or* effort

2 – needs improvement in quality *and* effort

1 – incomplete

Tasks	Done ✓	Points Earned
13.14 Compare and Contrast • List the similarities and differences between Winn-Dixie and Wilbur the pig on the Venn diagram.		
• Write a paragraph explaining the similarities and differences.		
• Include a topic sentence and concluding sentence.		
• Use details from both books to support your conclusions.		
13.15 Unit Project: Set Design • Complete the set design project for *Because of Winn-Dixie: The Musical*.		
• Use the rubric to score your set design. Record your score in the Points Earned column on the right.		
13.16 Review: Reader's Questions • Discuss your answers to the Reader's Questions from the beginning of this module with a parent, teacher, or reading coach.		
13.17 Book Talk • Use the suggestions to get a discussion going about the books your family or friends enjoy.		
13.18 Sowing Seeds • Talk about these ideas with a parent, teacher, or reading coach.		
Total		

Module 13: 180 points possible, plus 85 possible points for unit project

Checklist Point System:

1–6 points may be awarded by a parent, teacher, or reading coach for each task completed. Here are the recommended guidelines:

6 – exemplary in quality *and* effort

5 – exemplary in either quality *or* effort

4 – acceptable in quality *and* effort

3 – acceptable in either quality *or* effort

2 – needs improvement in quality *and* effort

1 – incomplete

Checklist for Module 14

Directions: When you have completed a task, make a ✔ in the "Done" column. Ask a parent, teacher, or reading coach to award you points for each task using the checklist point system. Fill in the points you have earned on the SLEUTH'S LOG in the appendix.

Tasks	Done ✔	Points Earned
14.1 On My Own: My Choice • Write the title and author of the book you have chosen to study.		
• Briefly explain why you have chosen this book.		
• Print an image of the book's cover and affix it to the space provided.		
14.2 Reader's Questions • Write at least five questions that you hope will be answered as you read this book.		
• Discuss your questions with a parent, teacher, or reading coach.		
14.3 The Cover of My OYO Book • Answer the questions about the cover of your OYO book.		
14.4 Meet the Author • With the help of a parent, teacher, or reading coach, research your author on the Internet.		
• Fill in the graphic organizer.		
• Print an image of the author and affix it to the space provided.		
14.5 Read Your OYO Book • Preview the activities in the unit before you read.		
• With the help of a parent, teacher, or reading coach, decide how much of your book you should read each day.		
• Write your schedule on the lines provided.		
• Read your OYO book.		

Checklist Point System:

1–6 points may be awarded by a parent, teacher, or reading coach for each task completed. Here are the recommended guidelines:

6 – exemplary in quality *and* effort

5 – exemplary in either quality *or* effort

4 – acceptable in quality *and* effort

3 – acceptable in either quality *or* effort

2 – needs improvement in quality *and* effort

1 – incomplete

Tasks	Done ✔	Points Earned
14.6 Word Sleuth: On Your Own • As you read your OYO book, fill the chart with new words to add to your vocabulary.		
• Make an educated guess about the meaning of each word and record it on the chart.		
• Look up each word in the dictionary and record its definition on the chart.		
14.7 I Spy Figures of Speech • List examples of figurative language on the chart. Include page numbers and types of figures of speech.		
14.8 Ruminate: On Your Own • Ruminate on the questions about the beginning of your book.		
• Discuss, draw, or write your answers to the questions.		
• Ruminate on the questions about the middle of your book.		
• Discuss, draw, or write your answers to the questions.		
• Ruminate on the ending of your book.		
• Discuss, draw, or write your answers to the questions.		
14.9 Review: OYO Fiction—Beginning • Review the beginning chapters of your OYO book.		
• List the new characters you meet on the chart provided.		
• Discuss your chart with a parent, teacher, or reading coach.		
14.10 Compare and Contrast: Openings • Compare and contrast the openings of *BWD* and your book.		
• Fill in the chart with details you collect from the opening chapters of both books.		
14.11 Setting: Where and When the Action Happens • Answer the questions based on what you learn about setting in the opening chapters of your book.		

Checklist Point System:

1–6 points may be awarded by a parent, teacher, or reading coach for each task completed. Here are the recommended guidelines:

6 – exemplary in quality *and* effort

5 – exemplary in either quality *or* effort

4 – acceptable in quality *and* effort

3 – acceptable in either quality *or* effort

2 – needs improvement in quality *and* effort

1 – incomplete

Tasks	Done ✓	Points Earned
14.12 Setting Constrains Characters • List three things the main character is able to do in your story's setting.		
• List three things that the main character is not able to do in your story's setting.		
14.13 Plotting the Plot • Discuss the events you will depict in each panel with a parent, teacher, or reading coach.		
• Draw a picture to represent an event that occurs during the most important stages of the plot in your OYO book.		
• Share your storyboard with your family or friends.		
14.14 Setting, Plot, and Characters • For each stage of the plot, explain how the setting influences the plot.		
• For each stage of the plot, explain how the setting influences the characters.		
14.15 Climax or Turning Point? • Discuss the ending of your OYO book with a parent, teacher, or reading coach.		
• Answer the questions about the climax and turning point in the story.		
14.16 Review: Reader's Questions • Discuss your answers to the READER'S QUESTIONS from the beginning of this module with a parent, teacher, or reading coach.		
14.17 Book Talk • Use the suggestions to get a discussion going about the books your family or friends enjoy.		
14.18 Sowing Seeds • Talk about these ideas with a parent, teacher, or reading coach.		
Total		

Module 14: 246 points possible

Checklist Point System:

1–6 points may be awarded by a parent, teacher, or reading coach for each task completed. Here are the recommended guidelines:

6 – exemplary in quality *and* effort

5 – exemplary in either quality *or* effort

4 – acceptable in quality *and* effort

3 – acceptable in either quality *or* effort

2 – needs improvement in quality *and* effort

1 – incomplete

Notes